HOW PARABLES WORK

Humphrey Palmer

Copyright © Humphrey Palmer 2008

All rights reserved; for permissions please email palmerparables@ntlworld.com
Table 9 may be copied without permission. And someone reading on-line may make one copy of any chapter.

Translations of Gospel parables are by kind permission based on *The Greek New Testament,* published by the United Bible Societies.

Details of other works quoted or consulted are given in Table 11, Books.

Comment on this book would be welcome; please email to the address given above.

ISBN 978-0-9558538-0-7

This book is published by the author.

To order through a bookshop quote ISBN.
To order online go to   www.lulu.com/uk
   click buy and book, then search on author or title;
   click below picture for a free Preview.

THANKS indeed ..

After study in Oxford the author taught philosophy in Cardiff University and in India. His puzzle and tussle with the parables has run up many debts, especially...

to members of seminars, in Tambaram, Cardiff, Gregynog and Leipzig, for responses encouraging and critical.

to Professors Christine Trevett, Martin Hengel, Hans Weder, Christoph Kähler and Wolfgang Harnisch for guidance and encouragement,

to AT Cadoux, CH Dodd, J Jeremias, JR Macphail and A Parker, for writing their books,

to <u>Novum Testamentum</u> 1977, <u>Modern Theology</u> 1986, and <u>Expository Times</u> 2000, for publishing articles,

to librarians of Penarth Town and of Cardiff University,

to Lorraine Woods for creating the front cover,

to Lulu.com and their web-flying Gurus, by whose aetherial guidance I may have submitted a printable text,

to Elizabeth, who had to put up with me and it.

CONTENTS

INTRODUCTION   9
About comparison, references, theories, capitals, and what this book is about.

I   ENGAGING THE HEARERS   17
The Teller proposes a Verdict, poses a question, invites reaction, speaks to 'You', adds emphasis or suggests a comparison. These interactive features encourage Hearers to confront his tale.
         Table 1   *Interaction in comparisons*

II   ARGUING BY COMPARISON   41
As in some catch-stories, indirect prophecies, fables and dream-debates. How Verdicts lead on to Judgments. How to spot non-comparisons.
         Table 2   *Gospel Stories and pictures*

III   STORIES   55
 A story is there to make the Verdict acceptable. Twenty-seven Stories, with their verdicts. Ten are told with judgments too.
Table 3 *Gospel references, Synoptic paragraphs*

IV   PICTURES   65
Forty-two pictures, with their Verdicts. Twenty have judgments provided. More suggested.
         Table 4   *Judgments given or suggested*

V   KEYS   79
Parables as puzzles. John's treatment. The secret words of J.Thomas. Allegory.
         Table 5   *Comparisons in Thomas*

VI   PACKAGING   91
In a few parables the judgment is given first. Others end with a moral. Some are told to disciples, or 'the crowd'. Some are replies.
          Table 6 *Reports of audience*

VII PEGS AND GROUPS   99
A peg clips a parable into the narrative. Others may follow, peg-free. Pegs may suggest judgments. (Lists of groups in K, M, L.)
          Table 7 *Group-leaders and Standalones*

VIII INCOMPLETE COMPARISONS   115
A parable had only one verdict. Few of them match reported situations in Jesus' life. Review of those still without judgments. How to guess.
 Table 8 *Judgments given, suggested, or guessed*

IX   RESULTS   135
 Our way of working fitted all the complete parables, and our guesses about those still incomplete. Grouping should be by judgments.

X   OTHER APPROACHES   147
Modern theories about the gospels. Recent approaches to the parables, based on Jesus being a Jew, on startling elements in some tales, on the gospellers as novelists, and on our freedom to interpret any text any in way we like.

XI   THE GOSPEL COMPARISONS   173
Fresh translations of all the gospel comparisons:
     from Mark, 173; Matthew 181; Luke 203.

vii

List of Tables

Tables 1 – 8 come in chapters I – VIII

Table 1	Comparisons showing interaction	30
Table 2	Gospel Stories and pictures	53
Table 3	Gospel refs, Synoptic paragraphs	63
Table 4	Judgments given or suggested	72
Table 5	Gospel comparisons in Thomas	90
Table 6	Comparisons told to ...	96
Table 7	Group-leaders and Standalones	106

        Mark's groups 101, Matthew's 102, Luke's 104

Table 8
    Judgments given, suggested, guessed at   133

Tables 9 – 12 come at the end

Table 9	Coding	228
Table 10	Comment	231
Table 11	Books +	232
Table 12	Parable finder	242

Introduction

EVERYONE KNOWS THAT JESUS TAUGHT IN PARABLES. But what is a parable, really? And how were they supposed to work? Were they illustrations of scripture, like those of some other Rabbis? Or coded messages, as Mark suggests, to be understood only if you hold the key? And did all those parables say more or less the same, or were they on different topics, one-off responses to varied situations, or advice to particular groups or individuals?

This book looks at certain recurrent features in the gospel tellings of the parables, to show how they were meant to work. This enquiry and its results will sometimes be called 'our theory', for short, although much of it is not so very new.

This Introduction considers several general points, to save explanations later on.

How Parables Work

1. the name parable

Some things we call parables are so called in the gospels; others are not. And some things we would not call parables are called that in the gospels: as *Doctor heal thyself*, a proverb; and learning a lesson from the fig (K13).

To avoid confusion, each scholar lists the items he is calling parables, then re-defines the term to match his theory and his list. This policy lets his readers keep their old familiar word, but suggests a new meaning for it; which they remember for a page or two, but then slip back to the older usage he was seeking to reform.

The parables themselves give us problems enough, without an extra debate about labelling. In this book, therefore, we shall mainly avoid the word *parable*, and refer instead to comparisons.

2. Comparing X with A

Comparisons bring their problems too. It would be nice to have a separate word for each of the items being compared, as we do have for the premiss and conclusion of an argument. But which item 'comes first', in a comparison? It cant be the resembling itself, for that always 'works both ways'.

And what is 'works both ways'? Well, suppose you were asked to compare a raven with a writing-desk. You would look for features which belong to both: for similarities. You might decide that a raven resembles a writing desk in being coloured and in occupying space. If so, a writing-desk must also resemble a raven, in just those ways. Resembling is symmetrical, it 'works both ways' like *sharing* or *being a friend*, but unlike *being brother to*, for John being brother of Jane does not make Jane a brother to John.

Still, it takes people to make comparisons, and they do lay hold of one side first. The comparer arrives with some A already in mind; sunset, or birdsong, or a bicycle, and then looks around for some other X, to compare it with. So while the resembling itself is unavoidably symmetrical, the activity of comparing may well have a direction, arrow-like. The Kingdom was once compared to yeast: which meant 'please use what you know about yeast to help you understand the Kingdom.' Not the other way about!

In most gospel comparisons the A-bit is taken from real life; so this is called the 'reality-part'. Then the Teller suggests his X-bit, to compare that A-bit with. So his X-bit gets called the 'picture-part' of the comparison.

3. References

Many books on Biblical subjects are difficult to read. The page is spattered with numerical references, which offer 'chapter and verse' for the statements made. Some words have tiny numbers perched on top, to spirit you away to 'notes' printed somewhere else. Some of these may be important, some just give page-numbers in other books; and you can only find out which do what by going there – and leaving the page you had been trying to read. And then? Well, when you realise you didn't want that note, then you must somehow clamber back to the page you mistakenly left. And you may find, on arrival, that you have 'lost the thread' and will have to begin your reading all over again. Chapter One, on this system, is 'often begun but never done'; and a reader who realizes what the book is doing to him may just give up and go away.

In the text of the present book there will be no 'foot'-notes, no tiny numbers swinging on letters to strain your eyes, no cross-references to distract you from what you were trying to read. There are a few notes at the end of a chapter, mainly about other books. Having by then read that chapter, you are well-placed to decide for yourself which ones to bother with.

Comparisons will be referred to mainly by name; a name traditional or obvious, and underlined: Good Samaritan. At first the chapter is given too, using L for Luke, M for Matthew, and therefore K for Mark. Where these run parallel a

Introduction

comma will show agreement, but a slash / will indicate disagreement. Full references for all the comparisons are given in Table 3, and again in Table 12 (detachable).

4. Theories and Evidence

Serious cooperative and historical study of the New Testament, not pre-determined by religious doctrines, has now been in progress for two centuries and more, and has generated a great mass of scholarly work on all aspects of the subject, and many fresh approaches to the parables. How much of this should we mention, and when?

One solution is to keep mentioning all the main approaches, whilst explaining one's own. This technique wards off reviewers, but may leave readers floundering. So we shall not often refer to other theories while setting out our own. Developments in New Testament study generally will then be sketched in Chapter X, with an outline of some approaches to the parables which conflict with ours.

5. Capitals

The book is sprinkled with capitals: Teller, Hearers, Verdict etc. These are not meant to be pious, or pompous, as though a big letter made the topic Bigger Still. But they do make a

How Parables Work

reference particular; to the Teller of that comparison, to the Hearers who heard it, and the Judgment it was meant to lead them to, etc.

6. This Book

This book is meant for gospel-readers of all sorts, wondering what these tales were for. A start is made by seeing how the Teller engages his Hearers in the business of comparison (ch.1). The general plan of parables is then described, with some help from the Old Testament (2). Verdicts of the Story- comparisons come next, with their Judgments if available (3). Pictures are similarly reviewed (4).

Various 'keys to the parables' are then considered (5). After that, packaging; introductions, morals, audience (6). Then pegs to clip tales into narrative; and groups to range several after a peg (7). Judgment-free parables receive special notice (8). Lastly we list findings so far (9); and review modern developments in Gospel study (10). Then all the Gospel comparisons are translated afresh, with a coding to indicate their main features (11).

NOTES to Introduction

Books and articles are cited by author and title. Italics are used for book-titles, and for journal-names.

<u>Names for comparisons</u> (3)
Matthew names two parables: the sower, and the tares (M13). Later readers made up their own names, mostly from the picture-part. Here are some of our names, and theirs:

Bigger Barns	foolish landowner
Half-Day Work	good employer
Keep Knocking	friend at midnight
Mean Debtor	unforgiving servant
Night Out	waiting servants
Only doing job	servants' reward
seed	patient husbandman
Smart Manager	unjust steward
Tenants Kill	wicked husbandmen
Two Men Pray	pharisee and tax-collector

Chapter One

The Teller Engages his Hearers

ANY STUDY OF THE PARABLES of Jesus should consider this point: How did the Teller intend them to work on his Hearers? Perhaps this question should be taken first, before going into details of the symbolism used, or guessing how the tales might have got altered before they were written down.

This book offers an answer to that initial and fundamental question, and seeks to show that this answer does fit all the comparisons that have come down to us.

How Parables Work

First we shall look at interactive elements. Many comparisons presented in the first three gospels contain little phrases which show the Teller engaging his Hearers to attend and respond to his tale. That tells us something of how his comparisons were meant to work.

Some think the parables were just pretty little stories, to help us appreciate Nature. Others, that they were deliberately puzzling narratives, which could challenge us to a Change of Life. Or might they be coded messages from the Other Side, with so much to tell, if only someone had the Key? Or were they after all something much simpler, just a likeness you could hardly deny, but which then lets you in for something much more serious.

This last opinion is set out more fully in Chapter Two. The rest of the book then asks if it fits all the gospel parables, and what follows if it does. The present chapter sets the stage by seeking out those interactive elements found in these comparisons.

And how do we spot a comparison? By noting diversion. Anyone using a comparison has to diverge from his previous line of thought, in pursuit of the other half of his comparison.

1. Engaging Hearers

Having thus veered off course he must later veer back again, to return to his theme. So diversion provides a marker, for picking out comparisons. We detect them by irrelevance.

1. Teller invites a Verdict

This chap planted a vineyard, fenced it, dug a well and built a tower, then let it off to tenants. Come harvest he sent a man for his share of the crop, but they beat him up and sent him back empty-handed. Another man got a thumping too. The next one was killed; and many others who went were flayed or done to death. The owner had only one left, his favourite son, so he sent him last of all, thinking 'surely they will respect my son'. But they thought otherwise: 'here is the heir, come on, let's kill him and we can keep the land'. So they killed him and threw his body out of the vineyard, unburied. What is the owner going to do? He will come and destroy those tenants, and re-let the vineyard to other. <u>Tenants Kill</u> K12,ML

What is the owner going to do? asks the Teller. *He will re-let the vineyard, and finish off those murderers.* In Matthew the Hearers provide this reply; in Mark and Luke the Teller gives it.

<u>Two debtors</u> *were both let off, as unable to pay. So which will be the gratefuller? The one who owed more, I suppose,* replies the cautious Pharisee.

19

Quite right says the Teller; and that goes for you and me and her, as well.   L 7

Another multiple-choice question rounds off <u>Good Samaritan</u>: *which of these three would you say became neighbour to the man that was mugged? The one that took pity on him.*   L10

Answer me this one. A man had two sons. He came to the first and said My boy, please go and work in the vineyard today. Shant, said the boy; but then thought better of it, and went. The father also asked the second son. Of course I will, he said, but never went. So which one did what the father wanted? The first, they said. Yes, said Jesus. And I see taxmen and prostitutes getting into the kingdom first, ahead of you. John came to you in an orthodox way, but you never accepted his message. They did. Even then you would not and accept it.   <u>Two Sons</u> M21

The sons give opposite replies to the same request. Each then 'repents', doing just what he said he wouldnt do : a pleasing conundrum. So which of them did what the father wanted? The one who said No, but changed his mind. This Verdict is given by the Hearers, on request.

1. Engaging Hearers

2. Teller asks what the Hearers would do
(A sabbath dinner, but this man with the dropsy turns up. Is it alright to make someone better on Sabbath? No reply. So Jesus heals the man and sends him off; and says to them If your beast fell down a well you would pull him out at once, even on Sabbath. (No comment!) <u>Your Ox</u> M12,L

If one of you lost just one sheep, wouldnt you scour the hills till you found it, then come home rejoicing. <u>Lost Sheep</u> L 15/M

What friend of yours would refuse to lend bread for an unexpected guest, even late at night? <u>Keep Knocking</u> L11

If your man comes in from ploughing, will you at once set him down to a meal? Or have him see to yours first? <u>Only Doing Job</u> L17

These questions expect a negative reply. Others invite a positive response.
If you plan on putting up a multi-story job, won't you reckon up the costs before you start? <u>Cost to Build</u> L 14

Won't a commander facing invasion add up the numbers on each side, before he fights? <u>Cost of War</u> L 14

How Parables Work

This woman had just ten pounds, and lost one of them. Isnt she going to get a lamp and sweep the house and turn the place upside down till she finds it? And then call friends and neighbours in to celebrate: I've found that pound that I'd lost. Which is how God and his angels celebrate when one sinner repents, honest it is.   Lost Coin L 15

3. Open questions posed at the start

Can you ask a bridal party to fast?
                    Fast later   K2,ML

How can Satan expel Satan?
                    Divide and Ruin   K3, ML

Input isn't unclean, only output is
                    Food and dirt   K7,M

Burgling someone? Tie him up first
                    First subdue   K3, ML

If your boy asks you for bread
                    Snake sandwich M7, L

Can one blind man guide another?
                    Blind leader   M15,L

1. Engaging Hearers

If only they'd known he was coming
Burglar L12,M
cant work for two masters   Two bosses M6,L

brambles dont yield grapes
Trees and fruit M7,L
Lamps are for lampstands, yes?   Lamp K4,L

Nobody patches an old coat with unbleached cloth, do they, for the new patch would pull away from the old, making the tear even worse. And people dont store new wine in an old bottle, do they? If you did, it would burst, and you'd lose both bottle and wine. New wine needs new bottles.
Spoilt coat and bottles K2,ML

4. Direct Address

Some comparisons are 'personal':
*Why fuss about the smut in your brother's eye, when yours has a bloody great plank in, which you dont realise? With that obstacle, how can you offer to take out his little smut? Take the plank out of your own eye first, you twerp, then you'll see properly to remove his smut.   Log in eye M7,L
Ask the boss for extra harvesters*
send more men M9,L
Lose your sight and you will be in the dark
Eyelights M6,L

How Parables Work

Agree terms out of court
<u>Last farthing</u> L12,M

Don't you water your cattle on Sabbath?
<u>Your Ox</u> M12,L

If your friend called late at night
<u>Keep Knocking</u> L 11

When invited to a wedding ...
<u>Top Table</u> L 14

When you throw a party..
<u>Cant Repay</u> L 14

Don't put pearls down for the pigs to eat
<u>Pig Food</u> M7

In all these the You figures in the picture-part. In others it comes later, in the application.

This judge in Somewheretown had no fear of God and never bothered what people said. But one widow kept coming back to court saying Give me justice against my opponent. And he was damned if he would. But later he thought, though I dont fear God or man, still she's such a nuisance I must decide her case, or she'll really do me in. And the Lord said You listen to this wicked judge. And won't God, who has been patient so long, give his chosen ones justice at last, as they cry to him day and night? Yes he will. It wont be long.
<u>Persistent Widow</u> L 18

1. Engaging Hearers

Now listen to me - you've got ears, I suppose
<u>Sower</u> K 4,ML

Now that's how you should behave
<u>Good Samaritan</u> L 10

Be like people waiting up for the boss
<u>Night out</u> L 12

If you cant be trusted with dirty cash
<u>Smart manager</u> L 16

Thats what God will do to you, unless
<u>Mean debtor</u> M 18

The riff-raff will be in ahead of you
<u>Two sons</u>   M 21

Yet other comparisons have two You's, one in the picture-part and one in the reality-part.

Watch out, keep awake, for you dont know when It'll happen. Remember that chap who left home, telling each servant just to carry on with his job; and the doorman's job was to keep awake, for who could say when the boss would turn up, maybe late on, or at midnight or cockcrow, or even crack of dawn. If he turned up suddenly he might catch you asleep. You - and everyone- must just keep awake.
<u>Doorman </u>K13

If salt goes off what can you salt it with?...so you be at peace with each other
<u>Salt</u> K9/M/L

25

How Parables Work

The fig tells you by its leaves when summer is coming; and these events show you what is just round the corner   Signs of end   K13,M

You wont give your boy a pebble to eat ...and your father above knows what's good for you.
                        Snake sandwich   M7,L

After all, if he'd known when the burglar was coming he could have stopped him breaking in. You too must be ready for the arrival of the son of man.
                        Burglar   L12, M

'Cloud in the bay, rain on the way'. So you can forecast the weather. But you are hopeless at forecasting events.   Signs of times   M16,L

You'll be stood outside banging on the door...seeing all our saints in there – and you chucked out.   Locked out L 13

Is a servant thanked for doing what he's told? Should you be, for keeping the commandments?
                        Only doing job   L 17

Direct address engages attention, making the Hearers feel part of things. It is reported with twenty-five comparisons.

1. Engaging Hearers

5. Emphasis

A faithful and sensible servant was left in charge, to give out the rations; good for him if that's how the boss finds things when he comes. I'm telling you, he'll be put in charge of everything! But if that wicked servant were in charge, he'd think 'the boss is taking his time', and start. beating up the others, feasting and boozing with the drunkards. Then his boss will turn up unexpectedly, carve him up and chuck him out to join the moaners and groaners outside.   <u>Two Stewards</u> M 24,L

Here *I tell you* is to emphasise a Verdict.

Don't even think of getting out
                            <u>Last Farthing</u> L12,M

I say he'll be more pleased with that one sheep
                            <u>Lost Sheep</u>

He will get up, I promise you; not to oblige his friend, but just for shame   <u>Keep Knocking</u> L11

Take it from me, the boss will roll up his sleeves and have them sit down, and wait on them
                            <u>Night Out</u> L 12
I say it's the taxman whose prayer was answered.
                            <u>Two Men Pray</u> L 18

27

How Parables Work

Sometimes the judgment also is emphasised: Luke has this in <u>Lost Sheep</u>, <u>Your Money Back</u>, <u>Smart Manager</u>, <u>Persistent Widow</u>.

6. Try This One

The Teller suggests some X for his comparison:
The folk of today? They're like children in the market-place, shouting across to their mates, We piped but you never did a dance, not even a tear when we sang the lament. <u>Kids at Play</u> L7,M
Here the application is spelt out in detail. Others come just as images for God's Rule:
think of seeds, nobody watches them grow
<u>Seed</u> K4

It's like a tiny seed growing big
<u>Mustard</u> K4,LM

It's like flour rising <u>Yeast</u> M13,L
like finding treasure in a field
<u>Found Treasure</u> M13

like spotting a really super pearl
<u>Found Pearl</u> M13

Prudent housekeeper uses both
<u>New and Old</u> M 13

Well-built, flood-proof   <u>Two Builders</u> M7, L6

These snapshots come in the sections on parables.

1. Engaging Hearers

In Matthew some longer tales begin 'The kingdom is like':

like a king's son's wedding
<u>Missing Guests</u> M22 / L

like bad plants coming up among the wheat
<u>Weeds</u> M13

like a farmer hiring harvesters
<u>Half-Day Work</u> M 20

like a man let off a debt but then putting the screws on someone else <u>Mean Debtor</u> M 18

like ten torch-girls at a wedding <u>Ten Girls</u> M 25

This fishing-trawl was netting fish of every sort. They brought it ashore quite full, and sat down to sort them out. The good fish went into jars. The rubbish – what you couldnt eat - was just chucked aside. And that's how it will be at the World's End. Angels will sally forth to pick out the wicked, throwing them in the oven to burn. Wailing there'll be then, and shivering with fear.
<u>Sorting Fish</u> M 13

....

How Parables Work

All the gospel comparisons have now all been reviewed, for signs of interaction between Teller and Hearers. Six different types of interaction were found. Let us count up their appearances.

TABLE 1

Comparisons showing interaction

	K+	L&M	M	L	total
1. q. re verdict	1	0	1	2	4
2. would you ?	0	2	0	5	7
3. open q.	6	5	0	0	11
4. direct address	5	5	2	6	18
5. I tell you	0	2	0	1	3
6. try this one	2	4	7	0	13
sub-totals	*14*	*18*	*10*	*14*	*56*
7. no interaction	1	5	2	6	14
TOTALS	*15*	*23*	*12*	*20*	*70*

K+ means found in Mark and maybe in M and/or L
L&M means found in L and M (but not K).
M means found only in M;   **L** = only in L.
This table counts *comparisons*. For a total of *interaction* some comparisons would need to be counted at least twice e.g. Lost Sheep.

1. Engaging Hearers

7. Comparisons told without interaction
The scribes and Pharisees said He eats with taxmen and sinners! Hearing this Jesus said Its the sick who need doctors, not those who are fit. And its sinners I came to call, not the good people
<u>Dont Need Doctor</u> K2, ML

Thirteen more are told without interaction:
<u>Queen of S</u> M12, L
<u>Men of Nineveh</u> M12, L
<u>Vacant Possession</u> M12, L
<u>Two Shopmen</u> M17, L
<u>Noah's Day</u> M24, L

<u>God's Garden</u> M15
<u>Sheep and Goats</u> M25

<u>Bigger Barns</u> L 12
<u>Beaten Less</u> L12
<u>Fig's Last Chance</u> L13
<u>Prodigal</u> L15
<u>Tell My Folks</u> L16
<u>Sodom Folk</u> L17

8. Mere convention?
Some seventy comparisons have now been reviewed for signs of interaction between Teller and Hearers. Fifty-six contained some interactive elements. What should we make of this plentiful engagement with the audience? Nothing much,

perhaps, for the phrases here called interactive could be merely conventional. A man who writes 'My dear Mrs Jones' is not to be asked how she came to be dear or whether she is truly his. These are empty, customary phrases, learnt at school to start a letter with. *Bardell vs. Pickwick* has already made this point.

We have all grown up with these empty greeting-formulae; they are part of our culture, - and the stuff that local jokes are made of. This instinctive knowledge may bring embarrassment, if we go abroad and expect the same conventions to apply: the phrase *mud in your eye* is better not translated word for word! Similar dangers beset us if we venture into distant centuries.

Yes, *Good Morning* is indeed empty of meaning. It does not really refer to the morning or describe it as good. It does not really *say* anything. But it does convey a greeting, which may lead on to something more. So it has a function, although it has no information to impart. And the verdict-requests, direct address and surely-not questions we found in the parables did have a function, though they did not add to the content of the comparison. Thus in <u>First Subdue</u> Mark has *No-one can burgle a strong man's house* while Matthew has *How can anyone burgle* and Luke says plainly *when a strong man armed defends his property*. All three *say* the same, but Matthew and Mark say it so as to invite response, as if it ended *Come on, now, what do you make of it?*

The comparisons we called interactive could have been told in some other way, but the interactive features clearly had an effect on the Hearers. These phrases, used to help in the first telling, might well drop out in later re-tellings, and even more so when that tradition was put into writing. Yet our written gospels have plenty of such phrases left. In some seventy comparisons only fourteen now appear without any signs of interaction.

9. What makes a phrase interactive?

There is nothing new or peculiar in a speaker interacting with his audience. Whenever we speak to others we expect them to listen, for a time at least, and feel miffed if what we say is totally ignored. When many are addressed all together a more formal claim may be made for 'a hearing', with a chairman calling 'Order please' and would-be listeners shushing those still chatting in the row behind.

In the gospels some comparisons are told to the crowd; some to disciples only, a few to named individuals. The interactive features suit this personal telling; a speaker can invite or provoke hearers and adjust to their reactions on the spot.

How Parables Work

In what ways, then, do these little phrases tend to engage the hearers and promote interchange with them?

<u>Here is a comparison</u> This tells us a likeness for something is coming next: for example <u>Yeast</u> is going to tell us how the Kingdom is. Now dough is sticky, warm and good-smelling, and increases rapidly from within. The comparison-warning does not say which of these features is also found in the kingdom, but the comparison does: *until all was leavened.*

<u>You.</u> *You are stupid. You know when a heatwave is coming. You'ld better be ready, like servants waiting up.* Direct address is always interactive. It gets one hearer to realize he does agree, while another sees that he doesn't. Both have now woken up, and are attending seriously to the comparison.

<u>You never, Which of you</u> These draw the hearers into the story, inviting them to consider what they would do in the situation now to be described.

<u>If, Can, People don't</u> Here the invitation relates to anyone, including the hearers: they must decide what to expect of 'anyone'; how would the plain man react, in that situation?

Formulae in these last two groups seem strongly interactive, inviting the hearers to do something definite, here, now. <u>You</u> seems moderately interactive, aimed at individuals, and demanding their attention. <u>Comparison coming</u> is mildly interactive; but more so if the hearers have to decide in what respect the comparison is made.

And having got the hearers engaged, what happened next? The Hearer was asked to give, or agree, a verdict on the tale. The whole exercise turns on their reaching agreement on this point.

Table 1 shows that the types of interaction are spread widely across all the gospel traditions. Which suggests that they were not brought in by this gospeller, or that source-document, and favours the unfashionable notion that they were there in the tradition even earlier.

10. Interaction variously reported

In a few comparisons two gospels have different interactions to report; we show this by a / in the reference.

<u>First Subdue</u> K and M consider someone *getting into the strong man's house;* L has *when the owner is armed,* and reports a regular bout.

<u>Tenants Kill</u> ends with a question. In Matthew the hearers reply, in Mark and Luke the Teller does.

<u>Trees and Fruit</u> M has *people surely don't pick grapes;* in L they just *dont.*

<u>Missing Guests</u> L begins *this chap threw a party,* and ends *none of those absentees shall taste my meal.* M starts with a king's son getting married,

and ends by bouncing a replacement guest, for unsuitable dress.

Lost Sheep M scores no interaction for *more pleased with that one sheep.* L scores twice, with *I tell you there is joy in heaven.*

Blind Leader M says *if the guide is blind*; L has *surely a blind man cannot guide.* With this instance we reach triviality.

Overall these variations are quite minor, and exceptional. The versions of Tenants Kill differ only about who answered the question. In Trees & Fruit and Missing Guests we reckoned Matthew's wording interactive, but not Luke's. In Lost Sheep and Blind Leader L has the interactive wording, not M. No general tendencies here! Only in Missing Guests do we find a substantial difference.

Thirty-six comparisons are reported in two or more gospels. In six of these we find minor variations in the interaction reported. Thus in five cases out of six the reporting of interactive features is stable across gospels. Even allowing for some copying between gospels, this stability suggests that these interactive features were there already, before the gospel-writers set about recording them.

1. Engaging Hearers

11. Interaction in other texts

We went looking for interaction in gospel comparisons. Is it also found elsewhere? We should surely study all cases, before claiming that those in our favoured group are specially significant. But finding interaction is not just a matter of spotting standard phrases, but of showing that they were used for interactive purposes, by a teller engaging his hearers to take some part in what he says. This may be difficult, and open to dispute.

Let us try looking at questions, and emphasis.

<u>Questions</u>

John's baptism: God-given, or man's invention?
                                               K11,ML

Whose is this face and motto on the coin?
                                               K12,ML

These questions 'return the serve', meeting a hostile enquiry with another question which puts the enquirer on the spot.

Is telling him he is free of sin any less trouble than asking him to walk?   K2,ML
Is it worth conquering the world, and losing your own life on the way?   K8,ML

What did you go to the wilderness to see?   L 7
Can you get taller just by worrying?   M6,L

37

How Parables Work

These points did not have to be made in question form, for a simple statement would *say* the same: *you can't get taller just by worrying.* But a question invites you to think on, and make up your mind. So questions like these are interactive in intent. They are not, however, very frequent, except in the comparisons.

<u>Emphasis</u>
In comparisons the phrase *I tell you* is used to commend a Verdict, or to enforce a Judgment (as in <u>Lost Sheep</u>). Elsewhere it backs up a claim which sounds unacceptable:
I'm telling you Elijah has already been   K9,M
If they kept quiet even the stones would shout
                                                    L19
Matthew has it fifteen times in his Sermon, underlining 'fulfilments' of the Law.

The comparisons show more interaction, having more need for it. And these interactions are features of speech, not of writing. A teller can interact with his hearers: note their reactions and respond. A writer cannot interact in this way with his readers, as they are not *there.*

From now on there will be fewer gospel references. Full chapter and verse for all the comparisons is given in Table 3 on p.63.

1. Engaging Hearers

NOTES to Chapter One

<u>Tenants kill</u> (1)
 Matthew, Luke and Mark all tell this story - more or less. Or are there three distinct stories, about the same people? Yes, if the differences outweigh the similarities. Here they don't.
Those little differences can still be studied, in the hope of discovering tendencies in their writers; e.g Mark tells stories of Nature, Matthew's are all human if rural, while Luke's are of the town. (Goulder "Characteristics ..").

<u>Interaction</u> (9)   is studied in various fields:-
Delamont *Interaction in the Classroom*
Martin *Negotiated Order of the School:* teachers striking deals with the taught.
Lofland ed *Interaction in everyday life:s*pecial moves for special people, e.g. milkmen.
Interaction may also occur between a reader and his book. (Iser *Act of Reading,* 107). But the parables of Jesus were not part of any written text: he was there.
See also
Bailey *Poet and Peasant*
Derrett *Jesus' Audience*
Barton "..Reader-Response Criticism"

Chapter Two

Arguing by Comparison

THE TELLER WENT OUT OF HIS WAY to engage Hearers in his tale, so they would agree his Verdict on it. Just how was that agreement meant to work on them? And what did he hope to achieve, by all this roundabout?

We look first at some dramatic interludes from the Old Testament. These share some features with the gospel comparisons.

1. Catch-stories

Prophet Nathan comes into court to plead for a poor neighbour, whose only lamb was taken for a feast next door. Without further enquiry David pronounces judgment: the offence is capital; compensation set at three more lambs. This judgment, says Nathan, applies to you (the king), who took Uriah's wife and had Uriah done away.

Plea-bargaining follows, by which the penalty is transferred to Bathsheba's new son.(2 Sam 12).

Here a made-up story is told for real, to extract a verdict from the hearer. The teller then says You're another; what you did is like what that man in the story did, and deserves a similar punishment.

Joab, David's Commander-in-Chief, has a scheme for bringing another son of David home from exile. A wise woman is sent in to pretend a family tragedy: one son dead in a fight, relatives clamouring to kill the other as a murderer; which would leave no defender for her, and no heir. David says he will see what can be done. Further bleating ratchets this up to a usable promise: *there shall not one hair of thy son fall to the earth*. She then claims the king has *convicted himself*, as his banished son is not brought back, as all would wish. (2 Samuel 14).

Here the promise relates to a fictional son, *so why not* bring back from exile the king's own son? David could have said he didnt promise that. But the tale did achieve something just by mentioning the unmentionable. Fulsome interactive O-my-Lord-ing is also provided (omitted here).

2. Arguing by Comparison

King Ahab defeated Ben-Hadad of Syria, then came to terms with him. A prophet said this broke his vow, on which the victory was won: no prisoners. This was conveyed in a tale of a missing PoW, which Ahab should judge - and be caught by (1 Kings 20).

These catch-stories are fiction told as real, to extract from the hearer a verdict which can be turned on him. This takes a little arranging. Verdict and judgment should be close enough to trap an unwilling hearer, but not so close that he sees it coming. Mustn't give the game away!

Were these clever fictions really told on the occasions mentioned, or made up later to point a moral and adorn a narrative? We do not know. But even a fictional fiction depends on the hearers knowing how this business works.

2. Indirect prophecies

Isaiah sings of a vineyard, cultivated but unfruitful, and therefore wrecked and abandoned. The last verse reveals who is meant - Judah and Israel(Isaiah 5). In similar vein Ezekiel denounces greedy and heartless shepherds who do nothing for their sheep (Ezekiel 34). No judgment is given: you have to work it out.

How Parables Work

Arguing by proclamation is very public, and for that reason the hearer (or victim) is less likely to be caught out. But the hearer is still expected to consider the picture-part first, and then to transfer this verdict to reality.

Jotham, sole survivor of a palace massacre, climbs Mount Gerizim to declaim a fable about trees who wanted a king. The olive refuses to *wave to and fro over the trees*, having better things to do. Fig and vine also reject the useless crown. But the bramble accepts, promising a forest fire if their support is not given in good faith. And you, you murderous lot, will get burnt for betraying your debt to Jerubbaal (Judges 9).

That fires may start in brambles, all can believe and no-one need dispute. Was it honourable to support Abimelech, the sixty-nine-times fratricide? Maybe not. But is that point enforced by a comparison with forest fires? Hardly, for they bring unexpected danger, whereas this judgment turns on facts well known in advance, and on memory betrayed. The fable does include a recital of recent unmentionable events, and this may have had persuasive effect. Interaction is provided at the start by addressing 'you men of Shechem', and by many 'you's' in the application.

2. Arguing by Comparison

There are not many story-comparisons like this in our Old Testament. A few items are called parables, but in another sense: when Job 'took up his parable' (27 and 29) he was just re-stating his case. The collection called Apocrypha, however, offers an interesting example and development.

3. A dream-debate

Esdras is bemoaning the sufferings of the righteous: they would have been better off unborn! (2 Esdras 4). He then dreams of an angel correcting him by a comparison: the trees tried to grow on the shore and the waves sought to flood their plain, but neither won as the woods caught fire and the waves got lost in the sand. So which was right? Neither, says Esdras, for the waves belong in the sea and the trees are at home on the land. Good, says the angel, you got that one right, so why can't you solve your own problem? You must realize that people belong herebelow, and can only understand earthly affairs. Heavenly matters are a reserved area, accessible only on a need-to-know basis. M. Y. O. B.

To a waking mind this may seem a strained comparison. Granted that trees belong on the land, etc., we might agree that people belong herebelow. And therefore cannot even think about Upstairs? The angel suggests this, when convenient. Of course if a dream-angel enjoys wideawake authority, then a pious complainer, if told to put a sock in it, may do just that. Esdras didnt, but then *Esdras*, like *Job,* was written to challenge just such bullying.

The phrase 'Why judgest thou not in thine own case' (4.20) recurs in Luke 12, after <u>Signs of Times</u> and/or before <u>Last Farthing</u>; seemingly to suggest how simple and easy it all is.

4. Verdicts and judgments

In these earlier comparisons the picture-part leads to a verdict which the hearers can readily accept; and the real-life parallel is expressed as a judgment. Someone who accepts the verdict is then under pressure to admit the judgment too, just because it is parallel. The teller is in charge throughout, manoeuvring the hearers into agreeing the verdict and then on to conceding the judgment.

These features recur in the gospel comparisons. They all lead to verdicts; many declare a judgment too. Some are directed *at* the hearers, addressed as 'You'. But they are not really caught out, for a hearer already knows the game, and expects to pay a price for listening.

2. Arguing by Comparison

The gospels also have trap-stories, wrestling bouts in Jewish theology:
If a widow remarries, whose wife will she be in the after-life?   K12, LM
Can David be Messiah's ancestor?   K12, LM

Here the question is meant to endanger the recipient, by posing unsafe or unacceptable alternatives. He must parry the threat by escaping 'in between', as in a dilemma. But these are not comparisons.

5. Forms of comparison

Some seek to distinguish different forms or types of comparison. Comparing the joy of a shepherd who found a lost sheep with God's happiness when a sinner repents is simple: Picture This, now Picture That. In another tale a traveller is mugged, then rescued by a foreigner: and hearers told *on your way then, that's what you must do.* Some say this is example, not comparison. Another pattern just provides a picture: *Think of a merchant, collector of fine pearls. Finding one that was superb, he sold all he had, and bought it. That's how the kingdom is.*

A mere illustration? No, for in all these cases an agreeable verdict is given first, and hearers are then led on to a corresponding judgment. They all play the same game: to persuade, nearly to compel, though not quite giving proof. This 'way of working' is our main interest, and can be seen in all the comparisons. Sub-divisions can be left to those who need them more.

Can we be sure, in advance, that all gospel comparisons work in this way, dramatic acceptable verdict enforcing unwelcome judgment by parity of reasoning? No, we cannot. And we can't *prove* that Jesus never used allegory, or borrowed an existing tale. For such general statements could only be confirmed by a review of all the instances.

The next two chapters will show that most if not all of the complete comparisons did work on the hearers in the way just described, and that others look as if they had worked in that way before their judgments got mislaid.

6. Positive and negative comparisons

In these persuasive comparisons Verdict and Judgment run more or less parallel; that is why a Hearer who has accepted the Verdict feels obliged

2. *Arguing by Comparison*

to accept the Judgment too. And in the great majority of comparisons Verdict and Judgment run *in the same direction.* Thus in <u>Good Samaritan</u> the Hearer commends him for being neighbourly, and is then told 'you too should behave like that'. But <u>Men of Nineveh</u> works the other way: it commends the Ninevites for repenting at Jonah's preaching, so as to get at folk of today, who also had a message of repentance *but did not repent.* Verdict and Judgment are still parallel, here, but point in different directions: a negative comparison. Such persuasion by contrast is also found in <u>Queen of South</u>, in <u>Noah's Day</u> and in <u>Sodom Folk.</u>

7. Compression

For a comparison to work, picture-part and reality-part must be kept distinct, for they belong to different areas of life. But someone re-telling a familiar comparison will know what is coming next, and may jump ahead, using words that belong in the reality-part while still engaged in narrating the picture-part. For some reason this is called Compression.

<u>Locked Out</u> has a butler closing and barring the door; after that you knock in vain. Some late birds try claiming acquaintance, *we ate and drank in your presence, and you taught in our*

How Parables Work

streets, but get the standard brushoff *Be off you criminals.* And those who repent too late will be locked out of the kingdom, condemned to watch Patriarchs marching in with Gentiles to the feast. Here the claims of acquaintance really relate to Jesus, who holds the kingdom-feast for patriarchs and prophets, in the reality-part; they hardly suit the butler who has locked the door, in an everyday picture about people getting home too late.

Something similar may have happened in Matthew's <u>Food and Dirt</u>:
No-one can get dirty by what comes into him from outside, its what comes out from inside that makes you unclean. And when he got home his disciples asked him to explain. Well, he said, you lot are thick! Surely you realise that what comes in from outside wont dirty you as it goes into your tummy, not your heart, and on into the drain.
This homely truth about spit and shit requires a parallel, but was taken to *mean* that no food contaminates, only dirty thoughts.

Some light in these dark places may be had from Psalm 23, where the Lord is 'my shepherd' *to the sheep*. The shepherd gets me, the sheep, to rest up on good grass, so I wont go hungry. He takes me to drinkable water, and guides me along right and suitable paths. Even those terrifying places will no longer bother me, for he has a stick to protect me with. Then, somehow, the song sidles back from sheep to songster and to priest. People accustomed to handling such allusive language may not have troubled too much about Tellers changing horses, even in mid-stream between picture and reality.

8. Non-comparisons

A reader who can spot comparisons can also detect non-comparisons. For example, some items commonly called parables are better read as straight advice: Dont go for the best seats, Dont ask your friends to dinner, Dont take a dispute to court:

Try to come to terms with your opponent while on your way to court, or you will be handed over to the judge and then passed on to the jailer. The, you'll have to pay up, to the very last penny, I say, before you can get out.   <u>Last Farthing</u>

This is sensible advice. Is it also a comparison? No. It can't be both picture and advice.

The comparisons were intended to persuade. In most cases this purpose is evident. A few may fail with us, because we cant see where they are going: try <u>Salt</u> or <u>Eyelights</u>. And we may, in the end, decide that they are not comparisons. But not now. For the present, debateable cases must be left in our list, until fully and fairly considered. Which comes later on.

9. Success and Failure

Teaching by comparison may not always work. The verdict should be obvious from the tale; but some hearers may miss the point intended for comparison. Telling stories in the open air to a mixed audience will involve further restrictions: no recondite Biblical allusions, please, for hearers could not lug the text around, if, indeed, they could afford it, and could read.

Modern scholars can take various further helps for granted : chapter-and-verse division, a book-lined study, journals and libraries, wonderful computer programs, instant access to other scholars living anywhere. Which may well hinder their appreciation of stories told to people who had none of them.

Once Hearers were hooked on the Verdict they would need guiding towards the Judgment the Teller had in mind. In a few cases the Judgment might be obvious to all; in many more hearers needed to be told.

2. Arguing by Comparison

10. Stories and pictures

In some comparisons the verdict is reached from a little anecdote, with human interest and a developing story-line. These we call Stories (with a Capital). Other verdicts are provided flat, without development. These we call pictures. Someone hearing <u>Prodigal</u> cannot tell at the start how the tale is going to end. So that is a Story. But everyone knew that fishers had to throw some fish away; so <u>sorting fish</u> is a picture.

Table 2   Gospel Stories and pictures

	K+	M&L	M	L	=
Stories	2	5	6	14	*27*
pictures	13	18	6	6	43
totals	*15*	*23*	*12*	*20*	*70*

Stories come in Chapter III, pictures in IV.

NOTES to Chapter Two

<u>Old Testament comparisons</u> (1)
  C.Westermann *Parables of Jesus in light of OT.*

<u>The 'way of working' from verdict to judgment</u> (5)
see Cadoux *The Parables of Jesus,* 56
Dodd *Parables of the Kingdom,* 23
Jeremias *Parables of Jesus,* 21
Linnemann *Parables of Jesus,* 18f
Parker *Painfully Clear,* 63

<u>No scissors please</u> (9)
Parables should not be torn out of gospels, listed and classified.(Gerhardssohn "If we do not cut"). Fair enough, on his view. But if gospels were first put together from clips of oral tradition, snipping and re-arranging might be helpful. See also
Bailey & Broek *Literary Forms in New Testament*

Chapter Three

Stories

THE STORY-COMPARISONS reported in our gospels all lead up to a verdict; some present the judgment as well.

1. What a Story does for the Verdict.

In these longer comparisons, with human interest and a developing story-line, the intended Verdict may not be obvious to begin with, but the story makes it so.

Suppose you had a hundred sheep and lost one of them up on the hills, wouldn't you leave the others up there and go hunting for the one that got lost, and when you found it carry it home in glee and call in friends and neighbours to a party, saying I found that sheep I lost! And up in heaven they'll be partying over one sinner who repents, not over ninety-nine good people who have no need to. <u>Lost Sheep</u> L 15 /M

How Parables Work

This story tells of a solitary and dangerous *wilderness*, where the other sheep are *left behind* to fend for themselves, while the shepherd goes *far off* searching for the lost one. *Finding it* he *carries it home* in triumph, and calls family and neighbours in to *celebrate.*

Yes, we now think, he deserved a party after all that agony. But without that build-up we might have responded differently. Why all this song and dance about one sheep, we might have said. That shepherd was only doing what he's paid to do. Give him a party and he'll be losing one a week!

So we did need the story, that touching account of the human reality of shepherding, to show what there was to celebrate. The story is there to commend the verdict, and to jolly us into accepting it.

This also explains the economy in story-telling. We might like to know the shepherd's name and family and date of birth, the distance from home to grazing area, the breed of sheep and the price of one adult sheep at market that year. And no doubt there are other points on which some hearers might like to be informed. But these extra details do not help to make the Teller's Verdict more acceptable, so in telling this Story he just left them out.

The Stories relate to familiar facts of life: harvest, weather, invaders, debtors, children's games. Each one leads the Hearers to some definite Verdict. A story told for

3. Stories

this purpose must make clear to the hearers what verdict they are being asked to agree, without yet showing where that agreement might be taking them.

The interactive features noted earlier all helped the hearers to pay attention to his Story. A few of them may also help us to work out the judgment they had to face.

2. Twenty-seven Stories and their verdicts

Each story has a verdict, a definite point made clear in the picture-part, and readily acceptable once the story has been told.

Mark

Sower   *harvest great though some seed lost*
Tenants Kill   *owner will punish them and re-let*

Matthew & Luke

Vacant Possession   *tenants bad, squatters worse*
Lost Sheep   *big party, when found*
Two Stewards   *boss will come and sort them out*
Your Money Back *where's the interest?*
Missing Guests *Will-come replaces No-show*

Matthew

Weeds   *cant be pulled up until harvest*
Mean Debtor   *do as you were done by*
Half-day Work   *overpaying Peter not unjust to Paul*
Two Sons   Shan't *did. That's what counts*

57

How Parables Work

<u>Ten Girls</u>   *too late really is too late*
<u>Sheep and Goats</u> *its what you do that counts*

Luke
<u>Good Samaritan</u> *the foreigner was neighbourly*
<u>Keep Knocking</u>   *he'll have to get up in the end*
<u>Bigger Barns</u>   *death upset his selfish plans*
<u>Night Out</u>   *wait up for the boss*
<u>Fig's Last Chance</u> *give it one last try*
<u>Locked Out</u>   *cant talk your way in again*
<u>Top Table</u>   *try slumming to get promoted*
<u>Lost Coin</u>   *big party, when found*
<u>Prodigal</u>   *party for long-lost son's return*
<u>Smart Manager</u> *quick move got him a place to stay*
<u>Tell My Folks</u>   *some just won't be told*
<u>Only Doing Job</u> *no thanks for obeying orders*
<u>Persistent Widow</u> *petition granted*
<u>Two men pray</u> *one asked forgiveness*

3. Ten Stories told with Judgment

Some stories end with a judgment, seen as parallel to the verdict, making it difficult to reject once that verdict is agreed. The judgment provides a closure, rounding off the tale and signalling a return to normal, factual speech: 'that's it, boys'.

A story told without any judgment feels incomplete, like a tune overheard and cut off halfway through. But some have reached us in that state.

3. Stories

In ten Stories the judgment is given:

This king decided to check his servants' accounts. Right at the start one was brought who owed him a hundred thousand pounds, which he could not possibly repay; so the boss gave orders that he be sold along with wife, children and goods, towards the debt. He knelt down and begged Give me time and I will pay it all. Feeling sorry, the boss released him and let him off the debt. On his way out the man bumped into another servant, who owed him one pound; caught hold of him and started to throttle him saying Pay me what you owe. And that man knelt down and begged him Give me time, I will repay. But he wouldn't, instead he went and threw him in prison until he repaid the debt. Then the other servants who saw it all were very upset, and told the boss. He called the first man back saying You wicked servant, I let you off all that debt, because you begged me to. Shouldnt you take pity on your fellow-servant, as I did on you? And in a rage he handed him over to the torturers, until he paid the lot. Which is what my heavenly father will do to you, unless you genuinely forgive each other. <u>Mean Debtor</u>

    Verdict: *do as you were done by*

    Judgment: YOU'LL BE DONE BY AS YOU DO

        (SMALL CAPS for a judgment *given* in a gospel)

<u>Lost Sheep</u>   *big party, when found*
<u>Lost Coin</u>   *big party, when found*
        GOD KEEN NOT TO LOSE ANY

How Parables Work

<u>Two Sons</u>   Shan't *did. Thats what counts*
       EVEN TAXMEN *DID* REPENT, YOU DIDNT

<u>Good Samaritan</u>   *the foreigner was neighbourly*
       YOU BE LIKE THAT FOREIGNER

<u>Night Out</u>   *wait up for the boss*
       YOU BE ALL READY TO GO

<u>Locked Out</u>   *cant talk your way in*
       TO DINNER, OR TO KINGDOM

<u>Smart Manager</u> *quick move got him a place to stay*
       YOU MAY BE NEEDING ONE, TOO

<u>Only Doing Job</u>   *thank servant, for obedience?*
       OR YOU, FOR KEEPING COMMANDMENTS?

<u>Persistent Widow</u>   *bad judge, good decision*
       GOD WILL DO BETTER

4. Four kingdom-comparisons

Three incomplete stories begin *the kingdom is like*. This sets a topic, so may suggest a judgment.

This farmer went out early to hire workers, agreeing with them on a pound a day, and sent them off to his vineyard. About mid-morning he found others standing around in the marketplace, unemployed, and took them on saying You also go to the vineyard, and I will pay you the fair wage. So they went. The same happened at midday and mid-afternoon. And going out again late on he found still more men there, and asked. Why stand there all day doing nothing? Because no-one took us on, they said. So he said You also go along to the vineyard.

3. Stories

When evening came the boss told his steward to call the men and pay them all, last in first out. These last all got a pound. Those taken on first got one too, but expected more. So they started grousing at the employer, These fellows only worked one hour, we did the hard work in the heat of the day. Is that fair pay? He took one aside and said My friend, I'm not cheating you. You agreed for one pound. Take it then, and go off home. If I want to pay them the same as you, well, its my money, isnt it? Or is it my generosity that's making you jealous?

<u>Half-day Work</u> o*verpaying Peter not unjust to Paul*
 all enter kingdom on same terms.

(small letters for a judgment *suggested* in the text)

<u>Weeds</u> *weeding must wait for harvest*
 judgment will come - at the end
<u>ten girls</u> *too late really is too late*
 you be ready, just in case

The twenty-seven story-comparisons all arrive at a definite verdict, and in ten a judgment is stated. Three more begin *the kingdom is like.* The other fourteen must be reckoned incomplete:-

K+   <u>Sower,</u> <u>Tenants Kill</u>
M&L <u>Vacant Possession</u>, <u>Missing Guests</u>,
   <u>Two Stewards</u>, <u>Your Money Back</u>
M   <u>Sheep and Goats,</u> <u>Keep Knocking</u>,
L   <u>Bigger Barns</u>, <u>Fig's Last</u> <u>Chance</u>, <u>Top Table</u>,
   <u>Prodigal Son</u>, <u>Tell My Folks</u>, <u>2 Men Pray</u>

61

NOTES to Chapter Three

<u>fussing over one sheep</u> (1)
    For Dodd, <u>Sheep</u> and <u>Coin</u> show concern at losses which others might consider trifling

<u>Synopsis</u> (3)
Texts arranged in parallel columns
    Matthew | Mark | Luke
showing how far they coincide.

    The next table gives Bible references for each parable, with a paragraph-number on the left from Throckmorton or Huck. These numbers indicate an item's position in the narrative.

    A comparison told in two gospels and at the same place in the narrative will have only one para-number; e.g. <u>dont need doctor</u>.
    One told at different points, like <u>first subdue,</u> will have two or three numbers. But to save space only one is shown here, with '+'.

Table 3
Synoptic paragraphs, gospel references

159 beaten less L12.47	181 Only doing job L17.7
156 Bigger barns L 12.13	185 Persistent Widow L 18.2
115+ blind leader M 15.14 L 6.39	37 pig food M 7.6
225+ burglar M 24.42 12.39	173 Prodigal L 15.11
169 cant repay L 14.12	87+ queen of south M12.42 L11.31
171 cost of war L 14.31	20+ salt K9.49 M 5.13 L14.34
171 cost to build L14.28	95 seed K 4.26
86+ divide, ruin K3.24 M12.25 L11.14	58+ send more men M 9.37 L10.2
222 doorman K 13.33	220 signs of end K13.28 M24.32 L21.29
53 dont need doc K2.17 M9.13 L5.32	229 Sheep and Goats M25.31
33+ eyelights M 6.22 L 11.34	119+ signs of times M 16.2 L12.54
54 fast later K2.19 M9.1 L5.34	174 Smart Manager L 16.1
162 Fig's Last Chance L 13.6	38+ snake sandwich M 7.9 L 11.11
86+ 1st subdue K3.27 M12.2 L11.21	184 sodom folk L17.29
115 food & dirt K 7.15 M15.11	102 sorting fish M 13.47
101 found pearl M 13.45	90 Sower K4.3 M13.1 L8.4
101 found treasure M 13.44	54 spoilt bottles K2.22 M9.16 L5.37
115 god's garden M 15.13	177 Tell My Folks L 16.19
144 Good Samaritan L10.29	227 Ten Girls M 25.1
190 Half-Day Work M 20.1	204 Tenants Kill K12.1 M21.33 L20.9
147 Keep Knocking L 11.5	169 Top Table L 14.7
65+ kids M 11.16 L 7.31	41+ trees & fruit M 12 M12.33 L6.43
20+ lamp K4.21 M5.15 L8.16	34+ two bosses M6.24 L 16.13
22+ last farthing M5.2 L 12.57	43+ two builders M7.24 L 6.47
165 Locked Out L 13.2	83 two debtors L 7.40
36+ log in eye M 7.3 L 6.41	186 Two Men Pray L18.9
172 lost coin L 15.8	77+ two shopmen M12.35 L.6.45
172+ Lost Sheep M18.12 L15.1	70+ your ox M12.11 L14.53
136 Mean Debtor M 18.21	158+ Two Stewards M24.45 L12.42
87+ men of nin M12.41 L11.32	88+ Vacant Possn M12.43 L11.24
170+ Missing Guests M22.1 L14.16	96 Weeds M 13.24
97+ mustard K4.30 M13.31 L13.18	98+ yeast M13.33 L13.20
103 new & old M 13.52	95+ Yr Money Back M25.14 L19.12
158 Night Out L 12.35	70 + Your Ox M12.11, L14.53
184+ noah's day M 24.37 L 17.26	

3. Stories

63

Chapter Four

Pictures

A PICTURE IS A COMPARISON without development or human interest; flat, like a snapshot. Many were taken from common life, and seemed familiar. Others were taken as familiar, in the way that proverbs are, and then treated as agreed. In other respects these pictures resemble the Stories. Each one suggests a verdict for the hearers to agree; and that verdict once accepted puts the hearers under pressure to accept a parallel judgment.

Many of the pictures are instantly acceptable, and need no tale or argument in support. No-one needs persuading that patching will spoil a coat, or that those in good health need not see a doctor. The catch comes in the judgment which is then put forward as parallel.

1. pictures and verdicts

13 in K +

dont need doctor	only sick people do
spoilt coat	patching worsens
used bottles	old bottles burst
fast later	groomsmen dont fast
first subdue	tie owner up first
divide & ruin	division fatal
lamp	lights are to see by
seed	growth hidden till harvest
mustard	tiny seed big bush
food and dirt	what comes out dirties you
salt	cant re-saltify
signs of end	fig heralds summer
doorman	waiting up is his job

18 in M & L

last farthing	settle out of court
eyelights	all you have to see with
two bosses	cant serve both
log in eye	take your own out first
snake sandwich	won't give your kid one
trees & fruit	good tree good fruit
two builders	well built, flood-proof
send more men	need more harvesters

4. Pictures

<u>kids at play</u> can't agree what to play
<u>your ox</u>   you rescue on Sabbath
<u>two shopmen</u> sound fellow, good stock
<u>men of Nineveh</u> repented at Jonah's call
<u>queen of South</u> came far to hear Solomon
<u>yeast</u>   leavens the lot
<u>blind leader</u> both end in ditch
<u>signs of times</u> you forecast weather
<u>noah's day</u>   never saw flood coming
<u>burglar</u>   may come any time

6 in M sole
<u>pig food</u>   disappointed and enraged
<u>found treasure</u> sold all to buy
<u>found pearl</u>   sold all to buy
<u>sorting fish</u>   chuck out the duds
<u>new & old</u>   householder uses both
<u>gods garden</u>   God weeds, of course

6 only in L
<u>two debtors</u>   gratefuller if let off more
<u>beaten less</u>   knowing disobedience worse
<u>cant repay</u>   hold parties for penniless
<u>cost to build</u> add costs up first
<u>cost of war</u>   first reckon armies' strength
<u>sodom folk</u>   carried on as normal

How Parables Work

2. Judgments given

Twenty-three of these forty-three pictures come complete with a judgment:

Learn this lesson from the fig. When its branches are supple and the leaves come out you can tell summer is just round the corner. And when these things start happening you will know that Day is very near. <u>Signs of End</u>

In our lists these judgments will appear under their Verdicts, in small caps.

5 in K +

<u>signs of end</u>   *fig heralds summer*
        THESE EVENTS SHOW END IS NEAR
<u>dont need doctor</u>   *only the sick do*
        ONLY SINNERS NEED HELP TO REPENT
<u>divide & ruin</u>   *division fatal*
        SATAN DIVIDED IS SATAN FINISHED
<u>food and dirt</u>   *what comes out dirties you*
        BAD THOUGHTS ARE DIRTIER
<u>doorman</u>   *waiting up is his job*
        AND YOURS

12 in M & L

<u>trees and fruit</u>   *good tree good fruit*
        BAD PEOPLE CANT DO GOOD THINGS
<u>two bosses</u>   *can't serve both*
        NOT GOD *AND* MONEY

4. Pictures

<u>two builders</u> *well built, flood-proof*
    Better do what I say
<u>snake sandwich</u> *won't give your kid one*
    God's an even better giver
<u>kids at play</u> *Can't agree what to play*
    You lot are never satisfied
<u>men of nineveh</u> *repented, at Jonah's call*
<u>queen of south</u> *came to hear Solomon*
    But you lot didn't
<u>your ox</u> *you rescue on Sabbath*
    Doing good on sabbath is ok
<u>signs of times</u> *you forecast weather*
    Why not events?
<u>noah's day</u> *never saw flood coming*
    Caught out on big day
<u>burglar</u> *may come any time*
    You be ready for the son of man
<u>log in eye</u> first see to yours
    Damning can rebound

2 in M

<u>sorting fish</u> *throw out dud fish*
    Dud-people too
<u>new and old</u> *housekeeper needs both*
    Kingdom-scribe will offer both

4 in L

<u>two debtors</u> *owe more, more obliged*
    Loved more, forgiven more

<u>cost to build</u> *reckon things up first*
<u>cost of war</u>   *reckon things up first*
      BEFORE JOINING
<u>sodom folk</u>   *carried on as normal*
      CAUGHT OUT ON BIG DAY

total 23 pictures with judgment given

3. Judgment suggested

Six pictures begin *the kingdom is like*. For <u>Sorting fish</u> a judgment is given, but not for the others. But mention of the kingdom tells us where to look.

This chap sowed seed on his field, went home, and stayed there, sleeping at night, up and about here and there in the day, and all the time that seed was germinating and growing, and he never knew a thing about it. The earth bears fruit all on its own, first the stalk, then the ear, and finally corn in the ear. And when the crop is ready he starts in with his sickle, for harvest has come. That's what God's rule is like.   <u>Seed</u>

Judgments merely suggested will be listed in ordinary letters.

4. Pictures

2 in K +
<u>seed</u>　　　　　　*growth unseen, harvest obvious*
　　　When kingdom comes, you'll know
<u>mustard</u>　　　*tiny seed, big bush*
　　　Kingdom could grow like that

3 in M & L
yeast　　　*leavens the lot*
　　　Kingdom pervasive
<u>found treasure</u>　　*sold all, to buy*
<u>found pearl</u>　　　*sold all, to buy*
　　　Kingdom worth everything

total 5 pictures with judgment suggested

4. You-picture
How great the harvest, how few the harvesters
Better ask the boss to send more men
Addressed to apostles, this shows which harvest is meant, and so provides the judgment:
<u>Send more men</u>　　*ask boss for more harvesters*
　　　only God supplies preachers

How Parables Work

Table 4
Judgments given, suggested or missing

Mark +	Mt & Lk	Matthew	Luke
told with judgment			**10S+23p =33**
dont need dr.	Lost sheep	Mean debtor	Lost coin
divide & ruin	two bosses	Two sons	Good Sam.
food & dirt	snake s-wich	sorting fish	Night out
signs of end	two builders	new & old	Locked out
doorman	kids at play		Smart mngr.
	your ox		Only doing job
	men of Nin.		Pers. widow
	queen of S.		two debtors
	signs of times		cost to build
	burglar		cost of war
	log in eye		sodom folk
	noah's day		
	trees & fruit		
judgment suggested			**3S+6p =9**
1. its like	yeast	Weeds	
seed		Half-day work	
mustard		Ten girls	
		found pearl	
		found treasure	
2. at You			
	send more men		
told without judgment			**14S+14p = 28**
Sower	Vacant possessn	Sheep & goats	Keep knocking
Tenants kill	Missing guests	pig food	Figs last chance
fast later	Two stewards	gods garden	Top table
first subdue	Yr money back		Prodigal
spoilt coat	last farthing		Tell my folks
spoilt bottles	eyelights		Two men pray
lamp	two shopmen		Bigger barns
salt	blind leader		beaten less
			cant repay

Totals 27S + 43p= 70

For some incomplete comparisons an *explanation* is provided. Others have a *moral* or other closure. These are considered later on.

4. Pictures

5. Drive-in comparisons

There are many even shorter comparisons. These come inside sentences, and do not have distinct verdicts or judgments; but do bring in some other area of life, with which some current matter is compared. But a hearer is not brought to a stop by the comparison. He can take it in his stride. All four gospels report such 'oneliners', with various speakers. Here are some from the Synoptic Gospels, said by the Teller.

Two fishermen are asked to *come along, I'll make mencatchers of you.* A tall order, given a humorous turn by the metaphor.

Another applicant is told he can't go home to say goodbye; a tough line softened, perhaps, by the mention of ploughing; furrows do go wiggly if you turn around.

Several are shorter and more obvious:
Those who do as God asks make up my family.
Can you *drink of my cup?*
You scholars *lock people out of the kingdom*
I must go to *the lost flocks* of Israel.
Shoulder my yoke.
I came to set the world alight; perhaps I have.

How Parables Work

And what does *yoke* stand for? The hearer must work that out. Usually he can 'catch the drift': *mencatchers* must be netting people in, *lost flocks* are those who strayed beyond the Law.

Some oneliners start with *as* or *like:*
I'm sending you out *as sheep among wolves.*
I wanted to protect you, *like a hen with her chicks*
If your faith were *as big as a mustard-seed...*

Others develop a proverb or truism:-
The vultures will gather where the body falls.
You will tell me Doctor heal yourself.
You gag on a gnat but keep swallowing camels.

Here then are fourteen mini-comparisons, from all the main lines of tradition. They all offer lively images as comment on some known reality already under discussion. The hearer is left to make what he can of them.

Oneliners also occur throughout the Old Testament, and in John and Paul and the bringer of Revelation. They can also be found, in abundance, in most other literatures and centuries. There is nothing distinctive in Jesus' use of them. But his pictures and Stories were thought distinctive by his followers, who could not compose their own, or mend or analyse those that they received.

4. Pictures

Are oneliners just very short pictures? No, for they dont sidetrack the hearers, and they dont have specific verdicts and judgments. And they aren't really arguing anything, just making something more vivid and impressiver.

One-liners will not be pursued further in this book. We have enough on our plate without them (there's another one.)

NOTES to Chapter Four

Your Ox (2)
A man with a bad hand is planted in synagogue to get evidence of healing on Sabbath. Jesus asks if doing good then is OK, e.g. getting your ox out if stuck down a hole (Matthew). No reply (K]. This exchange re-appears in Luke's tale of a man cured of dropsy. All these tales are here called <u>Your Ox,</u> for they are all about *you* and *your ox getting stuck.*

Two Debtors (2)
The one let off more will be more grateful; she was let off much; no wonder she shows such affection. This reliable argument is behind the recital of 'you didnt but she did', vv.44-46. *I can tell you, her many sins are forgiven. Her great love shows that.* This is a further argument.

Oneliners (4)
Westermann presents many comparisons and oneliners from the Old Testament. See also
   Beardslee "Uses of Proverbs in .. Gospels"
   Linton "Co-ordinated Sayings and Parables"
   Winton *Proverbs of Jesus*

4. Pictures

Summary of findings, Chapters Three and Four

Comparisons told complete with judgment
        10 Stories, 23 pictures   33

Told incomplete, but with *kingdom's like*
        3 Stories, 5 pictures   8
Incomplete, but aimed at;
        1 picture   1

Incomplete, with no hints
        14 Stories, 14 pictures   28

                          total   70

Chapter Five

Keys

SOME GOSPEL COMPARISONS strike us as puzzling. Perhaps they were meant to be.

1. Parables as puzzles

Listen here. This farmer went out sowing. Some seeds fell on the road; along came the birds and ate them up. Some fell on stony patches, with little soil, and soon sprang up but got scorched when the sun came up; with no root at all they dried right up. Other seeds fell among thistles, and these grew up and throttled them. And some fell on the good ground and grew up and swelled and gave a crop thirty, sixty or a hundred times what was sown. Now use your ears. <u>Sower</u>

How Parables Work

Mark has this comparison given to a large public audience, but without any judgment. It ends *now you work that out*. The disciples fail, so they ask him privately 'about parables'. Jesus replies:
You've already been given the kingdom-secret,
Outsiders get it only in comparisons.
They'll never spot it, however hard they look ,
Though they hear it time and again they'll never understand; or they might turn back, and find forgiveness.

A solution is then given: sowing is like preaching, the yield varies, in hearers as in soils. In both the final harvest is magnificent. He goes on *Think of a lamp, lighted to lighten, not to conceal. And what do people hide things for? Only so they can turn up later on. You work that one out as well. And mind how you go, for you'll get as you give. Only hav-ers get, you know, but the have-nots lose what little they had. Or think of mustard, so tiny, but growing into a bush big enough for birds to shelter in. And with many such parables he went on preaching the word to them, so far as they could take it in. And he never spoke to them except in parables, though he did explain all of them to his own disciples, privately.*

5. Keys

There are three different explanations here. All three explain why some comparisons are told without a judgment. The first says they are meant for outsiders; insiders already have the kingdom-secret they contain. The second says the secret they contain will be disclosed later on. The third says Jesus was then preaching only in parables and only some hearers got the message.

Why offer several explanations, different and incompatible? Mark could be handing on various solutions offered in the traditions he received. Or he could intend them for different sorts of parable:- <u>Sower</u> as a tale left up in the air, meaningless without expert help; <u>lamp</u> and <u>hidden thing</u> showing what comparisons were for; <u>seed</u> and <u>mustard</u> to throw light on features of the kingdom.

2. John's treatment

In the fourth gospel Jesus is not forever telling parables. He has many striking one-liners, and uses symbols to get us past ordinary earthly bread to its spiritual counterpart, never stale, more nourishing...that is, to Jesus. Mark explained <u>Sower</u> by asking Where do I come into this? John asks Where is Jesus in all this?

How Parables Work

Some of John's symbolic expeditions may derive from the comparisons: there was this chap who got caught climbing into the sheepfold, around the back when the door was shut; which showed he was a thief. Even the sheep knew he was a wrong 'un, and would not follow him. The proper shepherd comes in by the door, calls his sheep out by name and they follow him (He's Jesus). A door is for keeping thieves out, and letting the sheep go to and fro. (Jesus the Real door lets his own into the kingdom, etc). Poachers come to kill and destroy; but a true shepherd protects the sheep, even with his life (as Jesus did).

In this gospel everything is explained, much of it twice. The writer thinks we need telling, and are not to be trusted with a metaphor. So he does not report comparisons, complete or incomplete.

Some say that the meaning which John or Augustine saw in a tale was really there all the time, waiting to be seen. Which is true, perhaps, in the sense that today's crossword was there all the time, in the dictionary, though we came across it only today, in the newspaper.

Mark's suggestion is more plausible. Jesus did have disciples, and must have instructed them privately. And he did tell parables. Many of these have passed down in the church, some without

5. Keys

any declared judgment. If that was how he told them in public, still he could have told his disciples privately what they meant. Two generations later, when the gospels were compiled, there was considerable interest in these comparisons, but no mention of asking an apostle to complete those that were incomplete. Were they all dead by then?

In those tales that survived complete with judgment each comparison turns upon a single point. A shepherd holds a party on rescuing his lost sheep, and so will God for lost sinners. This comparison is clear before anyone starts explaining it. Which takes us back to our problem: if the complete comparisons are so clear and compelling even now, then surely the others must have been clear and obvious, in order to compel. So the judgment was given, when the parable was told. How could it get lost again?

3. D.J.Thomas and his Secret Words

Many gospel comparisons re-surface in a work now called *Gospel of Thomas*; a Coptic document found in upper Egypt and dated to the fourth century. *These are the secret words which the Living Jesus spoke and Didymos Judas Thomas wrote, and anyone who understands them will not die.* There are a hundred-plus sayings, mostly beginning *Jesus said.* Some are one line long, others nearly fill a page.

About twenty-eight of these sayings are comparisons; of these, all but three occur in the gospels. A few are very close in wording: Sower (in section 9), Luke's Missing Guests (in 64); others are just recognizable, eyelights (24). Eight occur in our Mark, eleven in L&M, five in Matthew sole, and one in Luke. Only four of all these are complete in our gospels: food and dirt (KM), burglar (LM), two (LM), and Lost Sheep (LM); and of these, only burglar is complete in Thomas. But then he was collecting *secret words.* Perhaps some he collected were secret (of unknown meaning) because they were incomplete. He does provide a closure for found pearl: *you also seek the mothproof treasure.;* and wraps up Missing Guests with *Tradesmen and merchants shall not enter my Father's place.* Moreover sorting fish (8), Bigger Barns (63), Tenants Kill (65), and yeast (96) all have *whoever has ears* added on. Of the ten kingdom's-like comparisons in the gospels, eight re-appear in Thomas, widely distributed.

This collection offers its readers a secret or hidden tradition known to few and grasped by fewer; but for those who understand, a deathless salvation. To us this collection overlaps with our gospels; which his readers may not have had.

5. Keys

Two or more centuries after our gospels were written, a separate and partly different tradition of Jesus-words had also survived, perhaps orally. The material found in both gives us some measure of the rate of change in such traditions.

4. This means that

An allegory is a story told in code. Each item stands for one thing or person, in another realm. Thus Mark explains <u>Sower</u> by saying he's *sowing the Word*; *the ones sown on rocky ground* are people who welcomed the gospel to begin with, etc. You get the overall meaning by working out what each bit was meant to stand for. The coding is specific to the tale: a solution which fits <u>Sower</u> will not solve <u>Prodigal</u> as well.

Let us now consider a code-breaker or churchfather called Jones who is trying to understand an incomplete comparison as half an allegory. He needs to find real things which these story-bits could be standing for; and then combine them into a parallel narrative. The two tasks interact, for while many things could be matched individually to the story-bits, only some of these would make up a plausible narrative in the reality-part.

Producing a solution in this way requires ingenuity, but not divine inspiration, or even genius. It is a particular though unusual form of regular intellectual work, like setting crossword puzzles. But to 'those outside' the result seems remarkable, even miraculous. That is why allegorical solutions win respect. The double-fit seems so unlikely; we feel it must be right, because it works.

Here at last is a conclusion we can disprove, from public evidence. For some eighteen hundred years good Christian folk have been using allegory to extract meanings from the parables. Over this period many parables have been de-coded more than once. But for each parable at most one of these de-codings could be right, so the others must be wrong. Just look how many solutions did fit so impressively well *and were wrong.*

Could the Teller have used allegory, in his parables? We cant say, off-hand. Well, did he? The only way to answer that is to seek for comparisons which appear to work as allegory.
A man sowed good seed in his field. But while his men slept an enemy came and sowed weeds along with the corn, and went off. And when the seed sprouted and bore corn the weeds also came up. So his men came to the farmer and said Sir, surely you sowed good seed in your field. Where have the weeds come from? He replied That's an enemy at work. So the men asked Should we go and gather

them? No, he said, you might pull up the corn as well, while gathering the weeds. Let them both go on growing until harvest-time. Then I will tell the reapers to put the weeds into bundles first and burn them, but to bring the corn into my barn.

<u>Weeds</u>

The disciples could not work this out, so a solution was provided:

sower = son of man, field = world, good seed = kingdom-people, weeds = devil-people, enemy = devil, harvest = end of world, harvesters = angels (and so on).

With all those equations, who needs a parable? But the story itself is realistic, even humorous, and conveys an clear message without any decoding.

<u>Sower</u> also has a realistic story, long and complex enough to allow Mark's allegorical treatment, but without requiring it. There is only one punch-line, at the end; a magnificent harvest-home for the Good Land crowd.

Modern scholars dislike allegories because some much-cited instances seem far-fetched, and because interpretation becomes so free, depending only on our memory and ingenuity in devising judgments to fit.

Earlier centuries welcomed this approach. "A great deal of mediaeval literature is allegorical

...(in) the allegorical way of thinking ... the everyday world is seen as an imperfect reflection of the divine world."

5. Keys and theories

Mark was puzzled by incomplete comparisons, and offers a key or two, or three, to unlock them by. John has another key, which suits his aims but none of the parables. Thomas puts together an anthology of incomplete comparisons, for private study and individual revelation. These interpreters brought their keys with them, never considering which comparisons they did not fit.

5. Keys

NOTES to Chapter Five

<u>secret words</u> (3)
A Gnostic or know-er claimed special knowledge. Of what? That we share a divine nature, though now locked up in a physical body. Realizing this can take us beyond death and life, says Thomas; hence his *secret words* and *deathless salvation* .
Pagels *The Gnostic Gospels,*
Wilson *Gnosis and the New Testament,*
Grant *Jesus after the Gospels,* iii.

<u>imperfect reflections</u> (4)
an exciting idea floated by Plato in *Republic V,* and still afloat. On mediaeval thinking, see Peck & Coyle *Literary Terms*, 133. For a taste, try *Quest of the Holy Grail.*

<u>allegorizing</u> (5)
Those who took parables as this-is-that stories might re-slant them accordingly, or *allegorize;* some see this tendency in <u>Sower</u>, and in <u>Tenants Kill</u>.
Caird   *Language and Imagery, ix.*
Brown   "Parable and Allegory Re-considered "

Table 5   Gospel Comparisons in Thomas

The first column refers to numbered items in *The Gospel according to Thomas*.

T63	Bigger Barns	L12.13
T34	blind leader	L 6.39, M15.14
T21b	burglar	L12.39, M24.42
T24	eyelights	L11.34, 6.22
T104	fast later	K2.19, L 5.34, M 9.15
T14	food and dirt	K7.15, M 15.11
T76	found pearl	M13.45
T109	found treasure	M13.44
T 33b	lamp	K4.21, L 8.16
T26	log in eye	L6.41, M 7.3
T107	Lost Sheep	L16.13, M 6.24
T64	Missing Guests	L14.16, M 22.1
T20	mustard	K4.30, L13.18, M13.31
T93	pig food	M 7.6
T73	send more men	L 10.2, M 9.37
T8	sorting fish	M 13.47
T9	Sower	K 4.3, L24.32, M 21.29
T47	spoilt coat	K 2.22, L 5.33 M 9.14
T47	spoilt bottles	K 2.22, L 5.33 M 9.14
T65	Tenants Kill	K 12.1, L 7.16, M21.33
T47	two bosses	L 16.13, M 6.24
T45	two shopmen	L 6, M 12.35
T57	Weeds	M 13.24
T96	yeast	L 13.20, M 13.33

6 Stories, 18 pictures.

Chapter Six

Packaging

CHAPTER THREE CONSIDERED the twenty-seven Stories, with their developing storylines and human interest; and Chapter Four the forty-three pictures, flat, with no tale to tell. The Stories showed most clearly the pattern and working of these comparisons, by Verdict and Judgment; the more numerous pictures often had a commonplace as verdict, hardly needing to be agreed.

From now on, Stories and pictures will be considered together; but Stories will still be marked by an initial capital. Any tales told complete with judgment will receive an asterisk.

Most of the comparisons work to a single plan: first, offer a verdict which hearers can be got to agree; then produce a judgment which they now cannot dodge. The verdict itself has no special relevance to the hearers; it comes in only to commend the judgment. The judgment is relevant, and important, and usually debateable.

How Parables Work

Each tale when first told must have included a judgment, or suggested it clearly enough for the hearers to cotton on. Their situation may have helped in this: their own position and background, and the things that were then under debate. These matters were all external to the tale he told, but were present and obvious to those hearers. Details of such matters are sometimes provided in our texts, and may have been remembered along with the tale. Or they may have been made up by gospel-writers with more comparisons than slots.

1. Judgment given first

Several pictures are said to show what the kingdom of God is like. Thus the mustard plant shows how great growth can come from tiny beginnings; which suggests, but hardly shows, that the kingdom also will grow like that. Yeast, Sorting Fish and Found Treasure and Pearl also work in this way. In these comparisons the Teller was really telling them, not asking them to work it out from the comparison.

Matthew has four Stories with this kingdom's-like introduction: Weeds, Mean Debtor, Ten Girls and Half-Day Work. These carry a clear message, no matter who is telling them.

Two Builders is about Teller and Hearer:
Someone who does what he hears me say is like that chap who dug down to the rock, when building his house. Down came the rains, up came the floods, the winds blew and

that house took a real battering, but it never fell, being built upon the rock. But that other silly chap built slap upon the sand. Down came the rains and up welled the floods and the winds they all blew; they smashed against that house, and down it came. My, what a crash that was! And that's how it'll go with you if you dont do what I say.

The message is Obey this preacher, if you want to avoid disaster. But obeying a preacher is not parallel to house-building. So the comparison itself has little force. It does illustrate the authority this Teller claims – and which his Hearers accept in the very next verse.

2. Morals and Closures

Some tales end with a 'moral', a make-do snippet of proverbial wisdom, to replace a missing judgment.

If you get invited to a wedding meal dont take a top seat, for someone grander than you may come, and the host will ask you to let him take your place, and you'll be moved down the bottom end, in great embarrassment. It's better to start by taking a seat down there, so your host comes and says My Friend, please take a higher place; which will raise your stock with all the other guests. (You see, those who are puffed up are heading for a comedown, but anyone modest is in line for promotion). <u>Top Table</u>

This moral also follows <u>Two Men Pray</u>. The tale itself comes nearer to *First and Last will swop*, now attached to <u>Half-Day Work</u>; and even to <u>Locked Out</u>* - which already had a judgment.

After <u>Lamp</u> we are told that *people hide things only to reveal them later on,* a remark true of treasures, but not of any lamp. Similar wise-isms follow <u>Ten Girls</u>, <u>beaten less</u>, and <u>Bigger Barns</u>. After <u>Smart Manager</u>* we meet *honest-with-pence will be honest with pounds;* a thought which that manager sorely needed, but of little help to us.

Whoever provided these closures must have thought that something was needed, and maybe these would do. The holes are real, but these closures do not close them. Why end an argumentative comparison with a truth generally agreed?

<u>Sower</u> ends *you'ld better all listen to this,* or perhaps *you with the ears, you work this one out.* The phrase recurs with <u>lamp</u> and <u>Weeds</u> (and in some manuscripts with <u>food & dirt</u>*); and Luke borrows it to help with <u>salt</u>. In all these it seems to be saying that the meaning is obvious.

Some of the larger collections are rounded off with a comparison. Matthew and Luke end their Sermons with <u>Two Builders</u>*. Matthew ends his enlarged section on parables with <u>New and Old</u>* Mark ends his sayings on Coming-Back with <u>Doorman</u>*, Matthew with <u>Sheep & Goats</u>, and Luke with a clarion call to stay awake.

3. 'parable'

Seventeen of our seventy comparisons are called 'parable' in one or another gospel.
He told them this parable. How can one blind man guide another? Wont both end up in the mud? <u>blind leader</u>
Luke calls this a parable, Matthew uses it as one.

6. Packaging

All three gospels apply this term to <u>Sower</u> and to <u>Tenants Kill</u>, and use it for the lesson of the fig, in <u>signs of end</u>; Matthew and Mark also use it for <u>mustard</u>, and for <u>food & dirt</u>*. Elsewhere there is disagreement. Only Mark calls <u>divide and ruin</u>* a parable. Among comparisons found in both Luke and Matthew, Matthew applies the name to <u>yeast</u> and <u>Missing Guests</u>, Luke to <u>burglar</u>*, <u>Lost Sheep</u>*, <u>blind leader</u> and <u>Your Money Back</u>. Of those found only in Luke, five are called parables; of Matthew's ten, only <u>Weeds</u>.

The term 'parable' is not found *inside* the comparison, except in <u>Mustard</u>; so it may have come from a re-teller or writer. Matthew often has *another parable* as lead-phrase when inserting one into Mark's narrative. Luke also uses it to warn his readers: 'take care, comparison coming'.

4. Audience

In our gospels some things are said to 'the crowd', others are given privately to disciples.

He used to teach by the shore. And a great big crowd turned up, so he sat off-shore in a boat, to teach them on the shore... and his followers asked him about parables, privately, and he said... <u>Sower</u>

Let us try collecting these, using T (Taught in public) or D (given to Disciples). Where neither appears, maybe the previous audience stays on stage until relieved (t or d). Items given to named groups or non-disciples may be reckoned as T, especially in Luke. He has <u>mustard</u>, <u>last farthing</u>, <u>eyelights</u>, <u>Lost Sheep</u>*, and <u>Your Money Back</u>

95

told to 'the crowd', while Matthew does not. But in other comparisons reported more than once the audience is usually agreed.

Table 6   Comparisons told to ...

Audiences	K+	L&M
agreed as D/d	0 / 3	2 / 8
agreed as T/t	9 / 0	7 / 2
Totals agreed	12	19
not agreed	1	4

From the nineteen agreed between L and M we could infer that these notes of audience were not put in by gospel-writers. Notes of audience were provided more often for public teaching than for private; and more often for pictures than for Stories.

Of the twenty-nine comparisons with audience specifically noted, fourteen are incomplete; Two Stewards and send more men (D); Bigger Barns, cant repay, fast later, first subdue, gods garden, Sower, Tenants Kill, Top Table, Two Men Pray, Your Money Back (T), and Luke's versions of blind leader and Missing Guests. An audience of a particular person or group might suggest a judgment; but most of these notes are rather general.

5. Aimed-at

Seventeen comparisons were found addressed directly to 'you' and, perhaps, *aimed at* 'you'. The first Hearers would not need this information, but later, told-again hearers would.

6. Packaging

I'll tell you this. If only the owner had known when the burglar was coming he could have stopped him breaking in. And you too must be ready and waiting, for the Son of Man will turn up just when least expected. Peter said Sir, is that comparison aimed at us or at everyone? burglar* The reply consists of Two Stewards and, perhaps, beaten less.

In Bigger Barns, Top Table, Two Men Pray and even in Lost Sheep* Luke says who was being got at. And all three gospels report that Tenants Kill was aimed at the priestly party.

Several more were given 'in reply' to some comment, and were mostly usually aimed *at* the party in question; dont need doctor*, fast later, divide and ruin* (KM)
your ox* (LM)
Two Debtors*, Good Samaritan*, Bigger Barns, Figs Last Chance, Lost Sheep (L)

Some of these also introduce groups of parables: a peg to hang a group on. More of this in the next chapter.

Notes of audience are really reports about *the telling of* comparisons. Such agreed notes could go back to the oral tradition. And the label 'parable' does not determine or add to the content of a comparison, but does mark it as non-factual.

A judgment given first was to explain a comparison. A moral put in afterwards was meant to plug a hole. So those explainers, or hole-pluggers, did realize that some of the comparisons they had were incomplete.

Chapter Seven

Pegs and Groups

MANY COMPARISONS ARE TOLD just after some relevant incident, as in <u>Divide and Ruin:</u>
Scribes from Jerusalem came down saying the prince of devils was on his side, helping with his exorcisms. He called the people together and gave a comparison in reply: How can Satan expel Satan? A kingdom torn by civil war cannot survive, nor can a family. Satan would really be done for, if he rebelled against himself. And a divided family would go to ruin. So if the devil has taken up arms against himself, that will be the end of him, he cant survive.

How Parables Work

Here the suggestion of working with the Devil's help gives point to the comparison, and also pegs it into the narrative. In other places comparisons are strung along, one after another, with no incidents in between.

A peg, then, is an incident or topic told just before a comparison and introducing it; as Dirty Hands comes just before food & dirt* in Mark, and introduces it, but salt, which follows Trippers-up, is not introduced by it. A group is a set of comparisons told one after another without narrative or incident in between. A comparison on its own, with no others following, is here called Standalone.

The following lists show the pegs, groups and standalones for each gospel. Items told with judgment still get an asterisk, and Stories keep their capital; but all lose their underlining, for clarity. Items found in Mark are italicized throughout; and those peculiar to Matthew or to Luke are shown in bold.

7. Pegs and Groups

1. Groups in Mark

ch., peg	comparison(s)
2 bad company	*dont need doctor**
2 fasting	*fast later, spoilt coat + bottle*
3 devils help	*divide & ruin*, first subdue*
4 parables	*Sower, lamp*
4 God's rule	*seed, mustard*
7 dirty hands	*food & dirt**
9 offences	*salt*
12 by what right?	*Tenants Kill*
12 s of man's Day	*signs of end**
13 dont know when	*doorman**

Fifteen comparisons, nine in groups. Group-leaders and standalones all have pegs. Twelve have a public audience.

2. Groups in Matthew

ch.	peg	comparison / group
5	sermon	*salt, lamp,* last farthing, eyelights, two bosses*, log in eye, **pig food,** snake sandwich* trees & fruits*, two builders*
	bad company	*dont need doctor**
9	fasting	*fast later, spoilt coat + bottle*
9	harvesting	send more men
11	baptist asks	kids at play*
12	sabbath heal?	your ox*
12	devil's help	*divide & ruin*, first subdue,* two shopmen
12	sign please	q of S* +men of nin*, Vacant Possn
13	parables	*Sower,* **Weeds,** *mustard,* yeast, **treasure + pearl, sorting fish*, new & old***
13	dirty hands	*food & dirt*,* **god's garden,** blind leader
16	sign pl. 2	signs of times*
18	dont despise	Lost Sheep*
18	peter asks	**Mean Debtor***
20	12 thrones	**Half-day Work**
21	by what right?	**Two Sons*,** *Tenants Kill,* Missing Guests
24	s of man's day	*signs of end*, noahs day*,burglar*,* Two Stewards, **Ten Girls,** Your Money Back, **Sheep & Goats**

7. Pegs and Groups

Eleven of Mark's fifteen comparisons re-appear in Matthew along with his peg and audience and position in the narrative; <u>salt</u> and <u>lamp</u> are moved to the Sermon and re-interpreted. Twenty-three more are found in Luke as well, but never in the same position. A further twelve come only in Matthew, making his score forty-eight, three times that of Mark.

Mark's three groups recur in Matthew, with additions. Matthew also has three further groups attached to standalones from Mark: <u>food and dirt</u>*, <u>Tenants kill</u>, <u>signs of end</u>*. His sermon has ten items, very miscellaneous.

3. Groups in Luke

Luke shares twelve comparisons with Mark, twenty-three with Matthew. Another twenty come only in Luke; nineteen being in his new Section (9-18), which includes six new groups, with pegs to suit.

Groups in Luke

3	bad company	*dont need doctor**
5	fasting	*fast later, spoilt coat + bottle*
7	Sermon	blind leader, log in eye, trees & fruits* two shopmen, two builders*
7	Baptist asks	kids at play*
7	dining out	**two debtors***
8	parables	*Sower, lamp*
10	preaching mission	send more men
10	lawyer's question	**Good Samaritan***
11	lord's prayer	**Keep Knocking**, s.sandwich*
11	devil's help	*divide & ruin*, first subdue,* Vac Poss
11	Jonah sign	queen of S*, men of nin.*, eyelights
12	legacy	**Bigger Barns**
12	dont worry	**Night Out*,** burglar*, Two Stewards, **beaten less**
12	peace?	signs of times*, last farthing
13	pilate's massacre	**Figs Last Chance**
13	sabbath heal	*mustard,* yeast
13	few saved?	**Locked Out***
14	sabbath heal 2	your ox*, **Top Table**, **cant repay**, Missing Guests
14	discipleship	**cost to build* + of war*** salt
15	bad company 2	Lost Sheep*+ **Coin* Prodigal Smart Manager*** two bosses*
16	law stands	**Tell My Folks**
17	faith please	**Only Doing Job***
17	son of man's day	noah's day*, **sodom folk***
18	(keep praying)	**Persistent Widow***
18	(self-righteous)	**Two Men Pray**
19	kingdom now?	Your Money Back
20	by what right?	*Tenants kill*
21	s of mans day 2	*signs of end**

7. Pegs and Groups

4. Groups and Standalones

In Table 7, group-leaders are those listed with a + ; standalones are shown without; a group is shown by naming the lead member with (+) the number of followers.

Most of the group-leaders are complete. So are most of the standalone comparisons. If, as seems likely, the gospel-writers compiled the groups, then they were also well aware which comparisons were incomplete.

In most groups only the group-leader is directly related to the peg. Table 7 shows the groups and standalones in all three gospels, with a number *before* each group, taken from Throckmorton's *Synopsis*. This number shows the position of a comparison in the narrative.

Thus fast later has the number 54 in all three gospels, showing that it comes at the same point in all three narratives. But kids, which has 65 in Matthew, 82 in Luke, comes at *different* points in their two narratives.

A little more about Synopses can be found in the Notes to Chapter Three.

How Parables Work

Table 7 Group-leaders and Standalones

K	M 18 salt + 9	L
53 dont need doc*	53 dont need doc*	53 dont need doctor*
54 fast later + 2	54 fast later + 2	54 fast later + 2
	58 send more men	139
	65 kids*	82
	70 your ox*	168
		73 blind leader + 4
	65	82 kids*
		83 two debtors*
86 divide & ruin* + 1	86 divide & ruin* + 3	149
	87 q of south* + 2	152
90 Sower + 3	90 Sower + 6	90 Sower + 1
	115 food & dirt* + 2	
	119 s of times*	160
132 salt	5	171
	133 Lost Sheep*	172
	136 Mean Debtor	
	58	139 send more men
		144 Good Sam*
		146 Keep Knocking + 1
85	85	149 divide & ruin* + 1
	87	152 q of south* + 2
		156 Bigger Barns
		157 Night Out* + 3
	119	160 s of times* + 1
		162 Figs Last Ch
97	97	164 mustard + 1
		165 Locked Out*
70	70	168 your ox* + 3
		171 cost to build* + 2
133	133	172 Lost Sheep* + 4
		177 Tell My Folks
		181 Only Doing Job*
	224	184 noah's day* + 1
		185 Persistent Widow*
	189 Halfday Work	186 Two Men Pray
	228	195 Yr Money Back
204 Tenants Kill	203 Two Sons* + 2	204 Tenants Kill
220 signs of end*	220 s of end* + 6	220 signs of end*
221 doorman*		

7. Pegs and Groups

5. Can pegs provide judgments?

How is it your folk dont fast, when John's do, and the Pharisees? So people asked. Jesus said The bridegroom's party would never fast, would they, not while he is with them? While he's there they just cant fast. Later on, after he's gone, that's when they'll fast. <u>fast later</u>

Wedding parties were exempt from fasting rules. The reply suggests that Jesus' party also was a special case.

<u>send more men,</u> in the context of a preaching mission, says only God supplies preachers.

<u>Tenants Kill,</u> in the final set-to in Jerusalem, proclaims that this lot just has to go.

<u>Keep Knocking</u> is applied by its peg to prayer, and says keep at it.

In the particular settings which these pegs provide, we can devise judgments suited to these comparisons:

groomsmen dont fast   WHY SHOULD WE?
more workers needed ASK GOD TO PROVIDE
owner will punish them and re-let
                   THEY'RE ON THE WAY OUT
keep knocking, he'll get up   KEEP ON PRAYING

How Parables Work

In <u>Two Men Pray</u> the Pharisee says a snooty prayer; clearly the bad guy. The verdict is stated with emphasis: Take it from me, that taxman was set right with God - as the hearers would like to be. So this must be a Youbelike:

        one asked forgiveness
      THAT'S THE WAY TO PRAY

In these five comparisons the context or peg helps us to arrive at a judgment - as it was probably meant to do.

Some pegs do not suit their comparisons. In <u>Your Money Back</u> the tale is about money, deposit versus investment, and the investor expecting some return. Luke says it is about God's rule; will it start tomorrow? A good question, for some other comparison.
<u>gods garden</u> and <u>blind leader</u> are not linked by topic to their group-leader, <u>food and dirt</u>, but
they do supply ammunition for the resulting debate with Pharisees, which could be taken as their peg.

<u>gods garden</u>   unplanted plants weeded out
        SO SHOULD GOVERNMENT BE
<u>blind leader</u>   both end in ditch
        AS OUR BLIND LEADERS WILL

7. Pegs and Groups

For <u>Trees and Fruit</u> Matthew offers a judgment at the start: beware false prophets! Luke has one at the end: only good people have good effects. Matthew also uses the punch-line in another place: if tree is good then so is fruit.

Mark retails fifteen comparisons, Matthew has thirteen of these, and another thirty-five; Luke has twelve from Mark, and forty-three more. Having somehow struck a rich seam of Jesus-comparisons, Matthew and Luke were keen to include these in their narratives; even those told without judgment, or reduced to scraps like <u>Eyelights</u> and <u>Vacant Possession</u>. Many must have reached them with no indication of time or occasion; to be shovelled into groups, with a lead-member pegged into the narrative. For items left over, special provision was made in the 'Sermons' of Matthew and Luke.

These arrangements may strike us as remarkable; not quite what we would have done, had we been on the job. But they do show these writers trying to preserve all the comparisons they had, and to fit them into their story of what Jesus said and did. They did not themselves compose comparisons, there is nothing to show that they could; nor did they convincingly complete those that reached them incomplete. They may have manufactured pegs; and some of these suggest completions, though these were not written into the text.

6. Can placing help ?

A peg is an incident or topic which introduces a comparison. May it also determine that item's position in the overall narrative?

send more men is given on a preaching tour, so must have taken place in Galilee;

Tenants Kill follows a dispute with high priests, so must come in the last fatal days in Jerusalem. If our three gospels have any historical backbone at all to their narratives, then these two incidents and the pegs they provide can rightly be used to help work out the judgments of these two comparisons.

In both Matthew and Luke Two Builders* concludes the Sermon, thus making a judgment evident: you pay attention to my teachings, or else! Matthew ends his group on parables with new and old*; here again the placing may help us reach a judgment: kingdom-scribes will bring out new treasures as well as old from their scriptures. If Two Builders came somewhere else it might convey a different point; but moving new and old would not make much difference.

7. Pegs and Groups

Other pegs precede incidents less firmly located in the narrative; <u>dont need doctor</u>* undermines an objection; <u>men of Nineveh</u>* rejects a request for a sign; <u>noah's day</u>* fits into a sermon on the World's End. But objections cropped up all the time; many people spent their lives looking for a sign; and the World's End was in their minds throughout this period. This loosens the link between these three items and their proposed timings.

7. Are gospel groups significant ?

Many incomplete comparisons appear in our gospels grouped with a complete one, usually as group-leader. Thus Mark records <u>first subdue</u> just after the judgment to <u>divide & ruin</u>*: if Satan also is torn by civil war, that will be the end of him. This placing may suggest that Satan needs tying up (first).

In both Matthew and Luke <u>two shopmen</u> is grouped with <u>trees and fruit</u>, to convey that bad people cant help saying bad things.

In Matthew <u>Missing Guests</u> comes just after <u>Tenants Kill</u>, so both may concern people dismissed as unfit. And after <u>signs of end</u>* there follow four more about people caught unawares; here <u>Two Stewards</u> might borrow a judgment from the other three.

111

How Parables Work

In Luke <u>snake sandwich</u>* says that as God is so much better than people, he will give much better gifts. <u>Keep Knocking</u> could also be a more-so argument About what? <u>snake sandwich</u>* does not say, but the peg does: requests in prayer. Luke also groups <u>Two Stewards</u> and <u>burglar</u>* with <u>Night Out</u>*. <u>Lost Sheep</u>* and <u>Coin</u>* commend a party for the long-lost now returned; as does <u>Prodigal</u>, which shows God waiting to forgive.

These hints suggest six judgments:
<u>two shopmen</u>   low shops sell rotten goods
    BAD PEOPLE CANT HAVE GOOD THOUGHTS
<u>first subdue</u>   first tie up householder
    SATAN IS TIED UP NOW

<u>two stewards</u>   boss will sort them out
    JUST WHAT GOD WILL DO

<u>Keep knocking</u>   he'll just have to get up
    GOD *WILL* ANSWER PRAYER
<u>Prodigal</u>   join party for son's safe return
    GOD WANTS ALL HIS CHILDREN BACK

<u>Missing Guests</u> if you wont come, others will
    SAME GOES FOR THE KINGDOM-FEAST

7. Pegs and Groups

Would it help if we re-grouped the comparisons by topic, from *all* the gospels? Grouping by the topic of their picture-parts would be easy, but pointless, for pictures on the same topic may lead to different judgments. Presumably parables should be grouped by their reality-parts; for that is what they are *about.* But we dont have all the reality-parts. So this re-grouping can be carried out only for complete comparisons -- where this help is not needed. How tiresome!

NOTES to Chapter Seven

<u>accommodating fresh material</u>   (2 and 3)
Luke and Matthew share 23 comparisons. <u>Lost Sheep</u>* and 5 pictures have the same peg in both; most of the rest go pegless into groups.

random groups (5)
Gerhardssohn in *Memory and Manuscript* tells of scribes using various odd features as memorizing aids, for matter auxiliary to the written Scriptures (151). This could result in seemingly random collections of material

peg-making (5)
A peg usually sticks to its comparison, wherever they appear.

trees and fruit (7)
Only a 'good' tree bears good fruit; which is a help when fruits are visible. What is a *good tree?* One bearing edible fruit. Then again you cant gather figs from thistles, can you, but only from fig trees. And what is Smith like, as a man? Only his actions can show. Perhaps we should accept this point without comparison or 'reasoning'.

Chapter Eight

Incomplete Comparisons

A COMPARISON HAS TWO MEMBERS, a picture-part and a reality-part. These must be distinct, or they could not be compared. In our gospels the picture-part leads up to a verdict, and a parallel judgment then sums up the situation in reality. Hearers who agreed the verdict feel that commits to them to the judgment too, by 'parity of reasoning'. For this system to work the hearers must know what the judgment is. If the complete comparisons are anything to go by, that means they would normally need to be told.

1. Complete and incomplete

Our gospels report thirty-three complete comparisons, with both verdict and judgment stated clearly. In the other thirty-eight the picture-part alone is reported. A few of

How Parables Work

these, such as Top Table, may really be narrative or advice, rather than comparison. Other tales, found in unrelated text, must be taken as half-comparisons.

How did our gospels come to contain so many incomplete, point-less comparisons:-
(a) did the Teller tell some without any judgment?
(b) did some judgments which he did tell then get lost, on their way to the gospels?
(c) did the gospel-writers leave out some judgments which they had received?

This last idea seems quite improbable. Luke and Matthew put together a substantial collection of extra comparisons for insertion at suitable points in Mark's narrative; providing some with an introduction to frame a tale, and others with a moral to round it off. And Mark put forward a theory about parables, which explains why some are incomplete. Writers with these concerns would not throw judgments away.

May we then suppose that the Teller often told a comparison without stating any judgment, leaving his hearers to work out what it meant?

Anyone with ears had better listen good   Sower

Someone planning a revolution might 'for security' leave hearers to work out what he really meant:
when you see these things happening you'll know It is very near.   signs of end*

8. Incomplete Comparisons

Keep your boots on and your lamps alight, as if waiting up for the boss to come back from the wedding, to open up for him at once when knocks. Those servants who are up and awake will really find it made; he'll put an apron on and sit them down and come along to serve their dinner up. They'll really have it made, I promise you, whether he comes late evening or after midnight.   <u>Night out</u>*

According to <u>burglar</u>*, the Son of Man will turn up quite unexpectedly. With no warning signs, so you just have to keep awake.

But only these few comparisons can be taken as revolutionary.

It has indeed been suggested that *all* the comparisons were originally told *in*complete, as their Hearers could tell from the situation what the message was. Later on, when these tales were re-told, explanations might be needed, and some were provided. This would explain why we have both complete and incomplete comparisons; but not why the incomplete ones were left like that

On the view presented in this book, each story or picture was carefully chosen by the Teller and so presented as to secure acceptance of a definite verdict which he had chosen in advance. The hearers were not to find their own verdict, but to agree with his, which would lead them on to the judgment that he had in mind. For this to work, he must have told them at some point where his tale was taking them.

Could it be, then, that some judgments got lost on their way through the oral tradition? This seems possible.

2. Effects of oral transmission

The tales which Jesus told would travel on among his followers, passing by word of mouth from A to B, and then from B to C, etc., complete with any changes they might have acquired on the way. Supposing there were many such transmissions, leading at last to Z, then this final recipient would have no separate contact with A, and no way of checking on the tradition he received.

The errors building up in repeated transmissions could in the end make a parable pointless, for example by dropping the judgment. Such a parable might well not get re-told. So the tradition Z received had been subject to two opposing tendencies, one reducing his stock of complete comparisons, the other culling some of those handed down incomplete.

The early form-critics (c.1920) tended to assume that each snippet would get passed on separately and many times; this was to explain the rounded form and disconnected sequence of so many gospel paragraphs. But if this repeated transmission took place in church-like situations it could also have a sifting effect; for items rendered pointless would not be many times retold.

If, however, the chains of transmission were rather shorter, with material reaching the gospel-writers after one or two re-tellings, then less change would have taken

8. Incomplete Comparisons

place on the way, and little or no sifting. In this case the last recipient should receive the original parables in good shape. Unfortunately we have no evidence how long these chains of transmission were, or even that they were all of much the same length.

Sifting – not passing on decrepit material – would require that you understand the material well enough to tell which bits are in good shape. The gospel-writers had rather hazy views about the parables, and may not have ventured on sifting; perhaps their predecessors had a more robust view.

At some point another and contrary process came into play. The early Christian community came to treasure any supposed 'word of Jesus', clear or mysterious. This meant that even an item as obscure as <u>Vacant Possession</u> could survive and eventually get written down - on the off-chance, perhaps, of some reader realizing what it meant!

Weighing these contrary tendencies one against another we may feel that prolonged oral transmission can hardly explain the loss of judgments from nearly half the surviving comparisons. And if there was a memory of Jesus teaching through comparisons, then those who tried to tell his tale in writing would surely have sought out some of those comparisons, complete, and might go on to collect other that were by then incomplete.

3. One Verdict Each

For a comparison to work it must have one clear verdict, for the hearers to agree. Even a conundrum like

How Parables Work

<u>Two Sons</u>* ends with a simple question requiring a straightforward answer.

Some say <u>Prodigal</u> has two.
So he made his way home; but his father spotted him some way off, and feeling sorry ran to meet him and gave him a hug and a kiss. So the son said his piece: Father, I have sinned against God and against you as well. I don't deserve to be called your son. But the father called the servants, Bring a robe quickly and put it on him, and a ring for his finger and shoes for his feet. And bring that calf we were feeding up for a feast, and butcher it so we may eat and enjoy, for this son of mine, who was dead, has come back to life, he was lost but now is found. So the party began.

Yes, a father might welcome back his 'bit of a lad' without comment. And when his brother complains of riotous unagreed expense the father again says, *your brother is back, as if from the dead.* These two verdicts are about the same thing, and say the same thing about it. That adds up to one verdict.

In <u>Missing Guests,</u> Luke has those who wont come to dinner replaced by others who dont mind if they do. Matthew achieves the same result by massacre, and then bounces a replacement, for improper dress. Or was this last bit originally a separate tale, <u>No Dinner Jacket</u>, with verdict *<u>decent dress expected</u>* and a judgment, perhaps, that souls need laundering, to get into the kingdom? (This shows how free we are, when devising a judgment for a comparison we have not got.)

<u>Prodigal,</u> then, has only one verdict. And <u>Missing Guests</u> has only one of its own - before Matthew set about improving it.

As we saw in Chapter 6, several incomplete comparisons were completed by adding morals or closures. Some of these do not suit the tale they have been fitted to, so are not worth counting as exceptions to the principle One Verdict One Comparison.

The single verdict intended for a tale must have led on to a single judgment. So where no judgment is given, we should seek out a single real-time judgment that matches the verdict. Several partial parallels will not do instead. We may of course consider several alternatives, before choosing: but choose we must.

A comparison with several judgments would not work. The Hearer is to accept the one verdict, as unavoidable; and then to confront one parallel judgment, as inescapable. With several judgments to choose between, dodging would be easier.

It is true that Luke trumps <u>spoilt bottle</u> with a wino's comment *the old is good.* But this is not a second judgment, but a wiseism offered in its place.

4. Occasions for comparisons

Attempts have rightly been made to fit the comparisons back into situations in the Teller's Life, by matching them to reported incidents in Jesus' ministry. Each comparison thus stapled into place could then be seen as a rapid response to some particular challenge: a tale told once only, on the occasion which required it; and later remembered by some of those present.

This would help to explain the scrappy state of the tradition, by reference to varying attendance, or to good or poor memories among those who did attend. But there is a serious shortage of Jesus-incidents suitable to serve as pegs. Are we then free to manufacture unrecorded incidents, to introduce our surplus comparisons? You cant stop novelists doing this sort of thing; you should not need to stop historians.

Some comparisons are reported as given *in response* to a comment: <u>dont need doctor*</u>, <u>fast later,</u> or <u>your ox*</u>. Here the comment serves to clip the item to a topic, not an incident. Luke has eight of these, Matthew one, KML two.

Pegs do not form part of a comparison. They were needed later, to help those who were not there. We have a good number of these helpful pegs, remembered perhaps, or guessed at as required. Are ancient guesses more reliable than ours? No-one will ever know. But at least those doing the guessing were nearer to the events.

We could also seek some general feature of the Ministry, as setting for the parables: Jesus was always preaching a Kingdom, so spare parables are probably kingdom-comparisons. This reasoning is very weak; but then some commentators are really desperate.

8. Incomplete Comparisons

Faced with an incomplete comparison, some are driven to wring meaning from its remaining picture-part.

This rich man had a really bumper crop, one year, and nowhere to put it all. What to do, he wondered. I know, I'll dismantle my barns and put up bigger ones, to store all my corn and stuff. Then I can have a proper holiday, a good time with plenty to eat and drink and enjoy. I've all that stuff in store, it'll last for years. But God thought different: You idiot, its tonight theyre coming for your soul. And who will all your stuff be going to? <u>Bigger Barns</u>

Here God's remark is part of the story. To match the tale to the peg, Luke starts with a moral against grabbing, and ends with one on the immorality of saving. These contributions relate only to the picture-part, showing it was all he had. Can we devise a judgment that really suits that Story? If not, we shall have to take it as illustrated advice.

Along similar lines, <u>fast later</u> could be seen as saying that the good times cannot last, and <u>Missing Guests</u> as requiring that even social obligations be observed. Embroidery on the picture-part is a harmless pastime, but unlikely to recover the missing reality-part, which was the real and only point of the original comparison.

5. Told only once?

It is hard to believe that long and precisely targeted tales like <u>Good Samaritan</u>*, <u>Ten Girls</u>, <u>Tenants Kill</u> were used just once and then thrown away, like paper handkerchieves. Instead, we may reasonably suppose that disciples were hard at it by-hearting these tales, along with the more formal sections of direct teaching, to help them pass the Message on. That, after all, was what disciples were for.

And this might serve to explain why some parts of the tradition are in a better state than others. On this view, the division into complete and incomplete could go right back to the original tellings: some were told to disciples to memorize, others were given to a crowd, some of whom might later try to recall the tale. A neat and attractive division, this, but not one that fits Missing Guests (L), Figs Last Chance, Prodigal, Smart Manager*, Sower, or Two Men Pray, which are all substantial but incomplete.

6. Completing incomplete comparisons

Although we don't know how some comparisons lost their judgments, we can still try our hand at completing them. A start was made on this, in earlier chapters, using hints provided in the text. Eight began *the kingdom is like*, showing where the judgment should be sought; and one is addressed direct to *You*, the hearers. Many more are set into the narrative by pegs; six of these were taken as hints. Six more judgments were based on parable groupings. That would leave fifteen unresolved. A brief study of these will round off our survey, and permit some reflection on how the guessing ought to go.

8. Incomplete Comparisons

7. Final judgments

<u>Sower</u> says sowing broadcast always involves some loss, but the overall yield is great.
>THE SAME GOES FOR PREACHING.

In <u>Figs Last Chance</u> a boss-man, tired of waiting for his fig to fruit, is persuaded to wait one more year.
>GOD MAY ALLOW YOU TIME TO REPENT.

<u>Tell My Folks</u> has a rich man tortured in hell for not helping his neighbour. Abraham says he can't interfere, and anyway its your turn to suffer a bit. Yes, but, could he kindly resurrect that beggar chap, to go and warn my family? No, if they disregard the scriptures nothing else would work.

This looks like a You-too story;
>YOU'VE HAD IT, IGNORING SCRIPTURES

You means you modern lot, as in <u>Kids.</u>

A <u>lamp</u> is lit to give light in the dark; even the dark cant make it invisible.
>PARABLES ARENT FOR SHEDDING DARKNESS WITH

In <u>Your Money Back</u> two are richly rewarded for profitable investment. *The third came and said Sir here is your pound. I had it wrapped in a cloth and put away, for I was afraid. I knew you were a tough one, taking what is not yours, reaping where you had not sown. The man replied*

You've said it, you wicked servant, you've condemned yourself. You knew I was a tough one, did you, one who takes other people's stuff, harvesting other people's fields. Why didn't you give the money to bankers, and I could have had it back with interest?

Here Number Three treats his pound as a deposit, so the boss takes it back, to re-invest. Fair enough, that's what he gave it for. Now the verdict is agreed.

The judgment must be about something meant to increase, like an investment; and not for hoarding up like a deposit.

<small>GOD'S WILL NOT LIMITED TO WRITTEN LAW (?)</small>

<u>Vacant Possession</u> may portray troublesome tenants, turned out then coming back in force. This could enforce a judgment about relapses after exorcism. But the exorcism-talk has leaked back into the picture-part; the comparison is 'compressed'.

<small>YOU CAN TURN A DEVIL OUT, BUT...</small>

Or is it straight talk about exorcism and relapse, from Jesus the exorcist?

<u>spoilt coat & bottle</u> say if your coat is past wearing, patching must make matters worse; and recycling old bottles is a recipe for mess. Make do and mend is a very bad policy. To what real-time matter could this be parallel? Some stare at the rotten old compromise government in Jerusalem, past caring for; a complete replacement is needed,

8. Incomplete Comparisons

GOD'S GOVERNMENT FOR GOD'S CHOSEN PEOPLE. We may mislike this comparison. We may think people should patch their coats, if they cant afford new. We may also think that 'Gods Government' has by now been tried quite enough, disastrously. But not by then.

<u>beaten less</u> may be about Gentiles and the Jewish law:
> ONLY THOSE UNDER THE LAW ARE BOUND BY IT

<u>eyelights</u> *The eye lets light into the body; a clear eye lights up the whole body but a bad one leaves it in the dark, real deep dark.*

If your eye is bad, nothing else can do its job. You have only one pair of eyes. Yes indeed, and one pair of legs, one nose, one reputation, one family.....
> YOUR ONE AND ONLY X IS INDISPENSABLE

<u>salt</u> is another 'one and only'; nothing else so spices a dish or preserves your meat. And nothing can do for salt what salt did for everything else.
> YOU NEED Z, IT ALWAYS WORKS

<u>pig food</u> Pigs do tend to get shirty. Dont annoy them, or get in their way! Is this aimed at moneygrabbers, who dont like criticism or obstruction?
> DONT CRITICIZE BANKERS!

last farthing says it's better to settle your case before you get to court; otherwise you'll probably end up in jail. If we cannot produce a convincing parallel we should leave this as straight advice.

Bigger Barns has yet to elicit a convincing judgment, so we must take it as advice (p.123).

log in eye says get your own eyes seen to first. Good advice to eye-doctors, of course, but always taken to imply a parallel criticism of some holier-than-him practitioners.

In Sheep and Goats a Son-of-Man is judging the Gentiles, sorting out bad from good *'as a shepherd sorts out sheep from goats'*. This little simile shows how to sort; the story itself says who will get sorted. The whole piece has to be taken straight, with a Oneliner tucked in on the way.

Top Table is set at a party. Important guests are advised to take a place down near the door, so the host will have to move them up *in front of everyone*. Which is scheming, not humility. As ironic advice, it adopts the self-regarding aims of these guests, and says You can achieve those aims better by this little dodge. No comparison.

cant repay *When you throw a party dont invite your friends, brothers, relations or rich neighbours, for they may invite you back and so square up the account. Instead you should call beggars, the disabled, lame or blind when you have a do, that way you will earn a real blessing, for they can't invite you back. Which guarantees a payback when the good people all come back to life.*

These are genuine reasons for having the poor to lunch: a real-life topic. There may be humour here, but no plausible picture, so no comparison.

Here judgments were proposed for <u>Sower</u>, <u>Figs Last Chance</u>, <u>Tell My Folks</u>, <u>Vacant Possession</u>, <u>log in eye</u> and <u>Lamp</u>, and suggested for <u>Your Money Back</u>, <u>spoilt coat & bottles</u> and <u>beaten less</u>. We can see what <u>eyelights</u>, <u>salt</u> and <u>pig food</u> are getting at, but not whom. <u>last farthing</u> is best taken as advice. <u>Bigger Barns</u>, <u>Top Table</u>, <u>Sheep and Goats</u> and <u>cant repay</u> are not comparisons.

8. Guessing by Rule?

If our texts tell us only the picture-part of a comparison, then the judgment can only be guessed at. If we wont guess, then we must throw the whole thing away. The picture-part by itself cannot teach us anything.

Guessing sounds rather reckless, too individual. Scholars call it conjecture. That sounds better.

Dealing with incomplete comparisons is one small part of scholarly study of the Bible. Work in this field requires a long preparation, and mastery of several ancient languages in unfamiliar writing. The worker needs a good head for details, to spot allusions across a thousand-page anthology, and to absorb and reckon with all the detailed contributions of other biblical scholars. The average reader may in consequence regard the biblical scholar with some degree of reverence, and be inclined to accept what he says; *he must be knowing, that's his job.* A touching thought. But then, a guess is still a guess.

Are there then any guidelines to which our guessing should conform, to make it respectable and reliable?

First, we should be able to recognise a comparison, or even half of one. We do this by noticing irrelevance; the picture has come in from nowhere, unrelated to any current topic or concern; so it must be the first half of a comparison. The picture itself is readily acceptable, without expertise. This helps to separate half-comparisons from non-comparative straight talk. Second, we must look out for hints at the area in which the judgment may lie; is it about salvation, forgiveness, discipleship...? If a gospel provides a moral or situation or an audience, a peg or just a grouping, then we should study them. Not that these were always right; but they are our only source of *information* on the parables. Third, our guess at the real point of the parable must be set out in a judgment, to make clear whether it follows from the verdict by parity of reasoning.

Mark retails a few comparisons, Luke and Matthew many more; in their extended versions of Mark, the extension is mostly parables. Perhaps they went around collecting those that people remembered, as folk-songs were collected in a later age. These collections of parables would of course need to be arranged, on some framework,

8. Incomplete Comparisons

and perhaps introduced or explained or rounded off by a proverbial saying in that area. The gospel-writers' efforts in this regard show them able to recognise incompleteness, and quite good at supplying closures; but not completions. (Join the club!)

To restore these missing judgments we just have to guess, taking what help we can from hints, pegs and groupings in the gospels. And the only test for our guesses is that mysterious, immeasurable quantity called 'fit': does the proposed judgment suit the verdict, and the Teller, and his ministry?

9. Whose fault ?

We have laboured long over missing judgments. Are these, perhaps, somehow due to the theory put forward in this book? That we first raised a dust, and then complained we could not see!

In many gospel comparisons there is nothing to show what they were about. That is a fact about the tradition, not a puzzle introduced by this or any theory

Our theory was about something else: in a comparison, *how* was the Verdict meant to persuade a hearer to concede the Judgment? This point can only be settled by reference to those told with a judgment. Where the judgment is missing we can either suggest one, or throw the comparison away. To arrive at a suggested judgment we do have to guess, and guesses are not evidence. But they may help decipher a comparison.

The following table adds the suggestions just made to those already set out in Table 3.
First, de-list five items now seen as non-comparisons:
<u>last</u> <u>farthing</u> (M&L)
<u>Sheep & Goats</u> (M)
<u>Bigger Barns, Top Table</u>, <u>cant</u> <u>repay</u> (L)

That leaves 65 comparisons. Of these, thirty-three have a judgment given, in eight more one is suggested, and in one derived from a You (see chs. 3 and 4); leaving 23.
Then we may find hints in the text. Thus in six a peg may help, as a group could, in five others; leaving 12.
Mere guesses provide possible answers for nine more; and the last three are left unguessed, although clearly significant.

Thus of sixty-five genuine comparisons sixty-two have been completed, well enough for us to get the point. The other three are clearly picture-parts of comparisons, but await some future reader to suggest their points.

8. Incomplete Comparisons

Table 8 Judgments given, suggested, guessed at

omitting Bigger B, Sheep & Goats, T Table, can't repay, last farthing.

K +	M & L	M.	L.
JUDGMENT		**PROVIDED**	**10S + 23p**
dont need doc	Lost Sheep	Mean Debtor	Good Samaritan
divide and ruin	burglar	Two Sons	Lost Coin
doorman	kids at play	new & old	Night Out
food and dirt	log in eye	sorting fish	Locked Out
signs of end	men of Nin.		Only Doing Job
	noahs day		Persistent Widow
	queen of South		Smart Manager
	signs of times		cost to build
	sna. sandwich		cost of war
	trees & fruits		sodom folk
	two bosses		two debtors
	two builders		
	your ox		
JUDGMENT		**SUGGESTED**	**3S + 6p**
mustard	yeast	Half-day Work	
seed		Ten Girls	
		Weeds	
		found pearl	
		found treasure	
	s. more men		
JUDGMENT		**HINTED AT**	**5S + 6p**
Tenants Kill	blind leader	gods garden	Keep Knocking
fast later			Two Men Pray
first subdue	Miss. Guests		Prodigal
	2 shopmen		
	2 Stewards		
	JUST	**GUESSED**	**5S + 4p**
Sower	Vac Possn		Figs Last Chance
lamp	Y Money Bck		Tell My Folks
spoilt coat			beaten less
spoilt bottles			
	UNGUESSED		**3p**
salt	eyelights	pig food	23S + 42p = 65

Hints by pegs 107f, by groups 112f.   Guessed 125f.

NOTES to Chapter Eight

unstated judgments (1)
"The parable is *all* the narrator says to his original listeners. They do not need an interpretation; they can understand the parable immediately from the situation". Linnemann *Parables of Jesus*, 24. A similar view is considered in Cadoux, *Parables of Jesus*, 19f.

by-hearting (5)
H.Riesenfeld in *The Gospel Traditions and its beginnings,* 16f, sees apostles as commissioned to memorize the words of Jesus, and recite them on formal occasions. Later on gospels were written containing those sacred words. See also B.Gerhardssohn *Memory and Manuscript.*

Top table (7)
In Proverbs we read "it is better to be told 'Come up here' than to be put lower in the presence of the prince" (25.7). This is clearly advice.

Chapter Nine

Results

WHAT GENERAL OUTCOME can be claimed, for this study? And how may it affect our understandings of the parables?

1. Findings, in detail

Many gospel comparisons include *interactive elements*, to engage the hearers in the tale. These do not add to the story being told, but do help towards the Teller's aim in telling it, by getting hearers to attend to his tale, and to agree his verdict on it. These interactive elements could also serve similar purposes in spoken re-tellings, but in the written gospels they are mere relics, fossilized evidence of an earlier stage in the tradition. From their presence in our texts we can reasonably infer that the comparisons reported in the gospels are not illustrations composed by gospel-writers, nor proverbs grown on into folktales by collective creativity in the oral period. Rather, these fossils of spoken interchange suggest that the texts they are found in can be traced right back to the time of first telling: to the Ministry (ch. I).

A complete comparison consists of a picture-part, leading to the verdict, and a reality-part, containing the judgment. Verdict and judgment run parallel, which puts someone who has agreed the verdict under pressure to concede the judgment as well. Our title *How Parables Work* suggests that the reported parables of Jesus all conformed to this pattern (II).

Is that really so? The Stories were examined first, those longer and dramatic comparisons. Here the suggested way of working fitted well, where a judgment was available. Some are reported without any judgment; but in these cases what survives strikes out an entirely fresh line, quite different from the texts containing them. Where such an odd bit is not straight teaching, advice, or narrative, it is probably the picture-part of some comparison (III).

9. Results

The pictures were shorter. Some had verdicts which were already known and agreed, such as proverbs. Less effort was needed in commending these. The complete pictures conformed to the proposed way of working; in most of the others, what is given is plainly irrelevant to any real and current concerns; showing them to be half-comparisons (IV).

This way of working requires a verdict which flows naturally from the picture or story, and is readily agreed to. A debateable verdict would not work, as it would concentrate thought in the wrong place.

Once the verdict is agreed the hearers are to confront the judgment. That was what the comparison was for, and what they were now poorly placed to deny.

Mark is puzzled by the parables being such puzzles, and presents some explanations then current. John just leaves out the parables, needing a clearer gospel. Thomas tries to collect them, especially those still incomplete, as secret sayings, worth salvation to the de-coder. None of this theorizing suits the actual process of the parables (V).

Sometimes a gospel comparison follows on some incident or debate, which serves to peg it into the narrative, and may indicate a missing judgment. A whole tail of further comparisons may then follow, some linked by topic, others just tucked in. The group-leader in these cases is almost always complete, and may help us with others in that group. The two Sermons provide larger groupings of this sort. Where an incomplete item ends up alongside a complete comparison this may have been meant to suggest a judgment. Other hints also are provided in the gospels, not always appropriate to the picture-part, but showing the writers' concern about missing judgments.

Some features of comparisons are fairly *stable*. Among comparisons reported in more than one gospel, *audience* is reported unanimously in thirty-one out of thirty-six (nineteen out of twenty-three in L&M). These notes of audience, then, were not put in by the gospel-writers, but found by them (VI - VII).

The interactive features also were quite stable (I). Pegs are moderately stable; of Matthew's nine non-Marcan pegs, five recur in Luke, though not at the same place in the narrative. So these pegs were there before Matthew and Luke began their separate projects of arranging things. Then if we look at items complete or incomplete: Matthew and Luke have the same ten complete in each, and thirteen incomplete, again agreeably. Thus the presence-or-absence of a judgment is a completely stable feature, in the only two gospels

9. Results

where this can be reckoned reliably. And the comparisons themselves do not vary much, between gospels. We are not reading different tales with similar names, but different versions of the same tale. Matthew and Luke do have differing judgments for <u>Lost Sheep</u>, and more substantial variation is found in <u>Missing Guests</u> and <u>Your Money Back.</u> <u>Salt</u> is given several completions, and <u>Your Ox</u> figures in two different tales (IV notes). That is not much.

The incomplete parables do present a puzzle. The Teller was careful to spell out his verdicts, not trusting his hearers to work them out. Surely he would take the same care over judgments. If so, those that reach us incomplete must have lost their judgments later on. Not that any gospel-writers would have discarded them, when they went to such trouble to collect parables and even fit them up with conclusions, if required. So the loss must have occurred in the oral period, between apostles and gospellers.

If transmission in this oral period was informal, multiple and ungoverned, then a lively picture-part might sometimes get re-told without any judgment, by tellers unaware of how the comparisons were meant to work. Might. The fact is, we dont know how these judgments got lost, or why the bits left over did survive (VIII).

2. A way of working

Anyone interested in discovering what Jesus was trying to do, in these comparisons, must first decide how he intended them to work. This book seeks to explain how his parables were to operate on the hearers, with agreed verdict enforcing unwelcome judgment by parity of reasoning. This way of working was found in all the thirty comparisons reported complete.

For a comparison to work it must have a verdict which the hearers will agree. The teller needs their assent to the verdict first, only then can he lever them into accepting his judgment. So the verdict needs to be acceptable on its own merits, without opposition or debate. No complex symbolism could come into this, no distant allusions, no hopalong chains of scriptural reference.

A comparison will convince only if Judgment and Verdict appear parallel. <u>Trees and Fruit</u> fails in this, despite several tries at saving it (7n). And <u>Two Debtors</u> has the answer back to front (IV.n). We would not expect to find many such failures, as those that failed would disappear.

This way of working can and should be applied to comparisons reported incomplete. That means finding a judgment which is parallel to the verdicts given. In some cases we failed in this

9. Results

search - then wondered if they were genuine comparisons: <u>Top Table,</u> <u>Cant repay,</u> <u>Vacant Possession,</u> <u>Sheep & Goats.</u> For the other thirty-six incomplete comparisons we did find possible judgments, using various hints and tips embedded in the gospel record.

Could the Teller have used comparisons in some other way, when he felt inclined? Maybe so; look at <u>mustard.</u>

What will God's rule be like? Think of a mustard seed, much tinier than other seeds, but when sown it springs up high beyond other vegetables, with branches so big that birds can shelter in its shade.

Here the picture-part shows that rapid growth is possible; suggesting it may happen in the kingdom too. The same point comes in <u>yeast</u>:
What is God's kingdom like? Like yeast, which a woman took and mixed into three measures of wheat flour, until all of it was leavened.

As the woman 'took it and mixed ...' the comparison is about rapid growth; not about tininess, nor stickiness.

In <u>Good Samaritan</u>* the verdict seems to be in the same realm as the judgment:
Which of these three would you say became a neighbour to the man who was waylaid? The lawyer said The one who took pity on him. On your

way, then, said Jesus, and mind you do the same. His judgment tells the lawyer to treat *other* cases in the same way. Here is a second realm, for the Judgment to occupy.

A similar point can be made about <u>Snake Sandwich</u>* and <u>Persistent Widow</u>*, where the argument from Verdict to Judgment moves 'from less to more'. These do all persuade, by reasoning from a parallel case.

The gospel comparisons must go back a long way. Those presented incomplete show the gospel-writers unable or unwilling to complete them. The comparisons themselves show stability in several features, taking them further back. And the interactive elements must come from the very first telling, as neither re-tellers nor gospellers had reason or wit to manufacture them

This book set out to show how the parables of Jesus were meant to work on their recipients. So it presented a verdict and judgment for each comparison received complete, and suggested judgments for most of the others. These verdicts and judgments exhibited our understanding of those comparisons and showed how this was affected by accepting the proposed 'way of working'.

When all this is done and decided, a further question can be raised: what light do these comparisons, thus understood, shed on the

9. *Results*

Teller's intentions, and his ministry? He hit on a novel way of conveying his message, and used it quite widely; perhaps that use will help to indicate what on the whole he intended to achieve.

3. What were the parables about?

Sower is a tale about seeds; some throttled by weeds, others trodden underfoot, and yet ... Convinced by this recital, the Hearers are to agree on the Verdict: *despite losses the harvest can be great.* To this we must find some parallel; something which could be great, despite initial loss. The Kingdom? Another tale tells of seeds, which the man sowed and then forgot about till harvest-time. This must concern something which comes to full development unnoticed. These two tales have similar verdicts but quite dissimilar judgments.

Here is *one* grouping of the comparisons by their reality-parts; the print shows a judgment as GIVEN, suggested, or <guessed at>.

A. What will the Kingdom be like?

new and old	KINGDOM- SCRIBE WILL OFFER BOTH
snake sandwich	GOD'S AN EVEN BETTER GIVER
mustard	kingdom could grow like that
yeast	kingdom pervasive

How Parables Work

found treasure +	
found pearl	kingdom worth everything
seed	when kingdom comes, you'll know
Two Stewards	<God will come and sort them out >

B. when will the Kingdom be here ?

doorman	YOU WAIT UP
divide and ruin	SATAN DIVIDED IS SATAN DONE FOR
signs of end	THESE EVENTS SHOW END IS NEAR
signs of times	CANT YOU FORESEE EVENTS?
noah's day +	
sodom folk	CAUGHT OUT ON BIG DAY
burglar	BETTER BE READY FOR SON OF MAN
Night Out	YOU BE ALL READY TO GO
Persistent Widow	GOD WILL DO BETTER
Ten Girls	you be ready, It wont wait
first subdue	< Satan is tied up now >
Keep Knocking	< God *will* answer prayer >
Figs Last Chance	< you've only one left >

C. who will get in, who wont

sorting fish	ROTTERS SORTED AND BINNED
Lost Sheep +	
Lost Coin	GOD KEEN NOT TO LOSE ANY
Mean Debtor	YOU'LL BE DONE BY AS YOU DO
Two Sons	THOSE WHO *DO* WILL GET IN FIRST
two debtors	LOVED MORE, FORGIVEN MORE
Locked Out	CANT TALK YOUR WAY IN
Smart Manager	NEEDING SOMEWHERE TO STAY

9. Results

Missing Guests	< no room for no-shows >
Half-Day Work	all come in on same terms
Weeds	judgment comes - at the end
Two Men Pray	< one found forgiveness >
Tenants Kill	< this government is done for >
spoilt coat +	
spoilt bottles	< and beyond repair >
beaten less	< demands on Jews heavier >
Your Money Back	< Israel, a poor investment >
Prodigal	<party for sinners returned>
god's garden	<God will start weeding here>
blind leader	<our leaders just as blind>

D. Kingdom - messages

dont need doctor	HELP SINNERS TO REPENT
cost to build +	
cost of war	RECKON UP FIRST
two builders	JOLLY WELL BETTER DO AS I SAY
Good Samaritan	YOU BE LIKE THAT FOREIGNER
Only Doing Job	EXPECT NO THANKS
kids at play	YOU LOT ARE NEVER SATISFIED
men of nineveh +	
Queen of south	YOU LOT DIDN'T BOTHER
your ox	DOING GOOD ON SABBATH IS OK
food and dirt	BAD THOUGHTS ARE DIRTIER
two bosses	CANT SERVE GOD AND MONEY
trees and fruits	GOOD ACTIONS NEED GOOD PEOPLE
log in eye	NEVER MIND MINE, YOURS WORSE
send more men	only God supplies preachers

How Parables Work

<u>two</u> <u>shopmen</u>	< judge people by their actions >
<u>fast</u> <u>later</u>	< why should we fast? >
<u>Sower</u>	< preaching will pay off >
<u>lamp</u>	< parables not to cast darkness >
<u>Tell</u> <u>my</u> <u>Folks</u>	< you also ignore scripture >
<u>Bigger</u> <u>Barns</u>	< private plans come unstuck >
	E. point unclear
<u>salt</u>	X also no good when stale
<u>eyelights</u>	look after X, no spares
<u>pig food</u>	dont preach to bankers

Eight comparisons describe the kingdom, thirteen discuss when it will come, twenty discuss who will or wont get in. The fourth group has items on disciples' behaviour, on law revisions, and on ways of conveying the message; most have some connection with the kingdom. Jesus clearly found parables a good way to talk about the kingdom. For other matters, there were other forms of speech and reasoning.

146

Chapter Ten

Other Approaches to the Parables

EARLIER CHAPTERS OF THIS BOOK presented one view of how the parables of Jesus were meant to work; reviewing them for signs of interaction with the hearers, and again for concluding judgments, for pegs used to locate them in the gospel narrative, and for the groupings those pegs introduced.

Other approaches to the parables were not presented or considered, in those chapters; for neither writer nor reader can do two things at once, not properly.

To make up for these omissions, the present chapter will offer a brief sketch of modern developments in New Testament study, and of some other approaches to the parables.

1. New Testament Criticism

In common speech, *criticism* means pointing out defects; though it can include pointing out virtues too. Thus a dramatic critic offers to tell us if the play is bad *or good*. And a Biblical critic is one who tries to see those ancient writings as they really were, in all their virtues and defects; and to make out when they were written, by whom, and why.

First he must try to establish what each author actually wrote; for their texts have come to us mainly by hand-copying, a process certain to produce mistakes, and sometimes worsened by efforts at correcting them. Here he must decide which are the oldest surviving copies, and how they relate to the original. In this task of Textual Criticism the methods first worked out for Greek and Roman classics have rightly been applied to biblical books; making due allowance for the much greater number of surviving hand-copies, for a more continuous tradition of scholarship, and for the copyists knowing much of their text by heart. These factors make the critic's task,

10. Other Approaches

where required, more difficult, but they did help to preserve the text.

A Textual Critic in this area needs to know several ancient languages, and to have a prodigious memory, and a very methodical mind-set. By devoted labours text-critics of the New Testament now have a pretty reliable text to offer, and only minor details to debate. All the other departments of New Testament study depend on that initial achievement.

2. Related documents

We do not know who wrote the gospels, or when, for the names they now carry are not in the earliest manuscripts. Dating has to work from Gallio, a Roman official mentioned in Luke's second book (Acts 18.12); and from Pilate's years of office. Some also hold that events presented as yet to come had usually happened already, letting the author know what to 'predict'. Thus when Luke (20) has a 'prophecy' of *Jerusalem surrounded by armies, this* shows that his book was written after 70 AD.

Further progress in dating depends on deciding which gospel was written first. Matthew Mark and Luke are very often found telling the same story, and in much the same words, and often at just the same point in the overall narrative. When these 'parallel passages' are printed out in parallel (as in a Synopsis) it looks very much as if somebody was borrowing. The study of such relations between books is called Source-Criticism, for if B takes matter from A then A's work was a source for B.

After much work and many theories it was quite generally agreed that Mark was a source for the other two. Another document (now lost) was then proposed to explain the bits found in both Matthew and Luke (but not Mark). To account for the remaining items (found only in Matthew, or only in Luke), two further writings were called into being: all together these would make up a 'Four-Document Hypothesis'.

Why were scholars so keen to unearth lost *documents*? Once borrowing was proved it seemed unlikely that the gospel-writers had got their information directly from the first disciples. Some chain of tradition was felt necessary, preferably in writing, to link the gospels back to the facts they narrate. Written sources lying behind existing documents would be the best way to bridge that gap.

The arguments for Mark being a source for Luke and Matthew continue to convince; but the material common to the non-Marcan parts of Luke and Matthew might be just snippets, handed down separately, by word of mouth (and now stuck together as a 'document', about 1885!)

10. Other Approaches

Does this matter, so long as we do have the material? Well, it leaves us with fewer documents to invent. And makes it harder to settle the aim or date or authorship of each snippet of tradition. This point is general, and is often overlooked.

Suppose we dug up an ancient document, in Hebrew writing, and referring to events during the captivity in Babylon. Hints and mistakes and turns of phrase from here and there in that book might help us date the whole and decide who wrote it and what for. For those bits and pieces all hang together. It's a *book*.

In an assemblage of oral traditions, however, the position is rather different. Here the features of one little item, e.g. its date or author, are evidence only about that item, and may not apply to the collection as a whole.

3. Oral Traditions

The first three gospels are largely made up of short, separate paragraphs, with no dates, few names, and not many places. This suggests that these snippets reached the gospel-writers by word of mouth, perhaps after repeated transmissions in that way. These possibilities were rather fully investigated by the 'Form'-Critics, so-called because they expected the *form* of the material to betray its history. In particular, the unusual form of gospel writings, with small rounded items and little structure or connection, was thought to result from their being passed on many times, by word of mouth, between people we know nothing else about.

When stories and messages are passed on in this way some errors will result. In written transmission these errors mostly come when a fresh copy is being made, perhaps after a century or more. But what A says to B may be repeated next day by B to C; and so on. So matter passed on orally could be passed on many times, before a document got copied once. Changes may also occur in between transmissions, when the holder reflects on the material, or mixes in new items remembered from elsewhere.

The period of oral transmission thought to have come between apostles and gospellers was relatively brief: a generation or so. As so little is known about this period, critics tended to adopt a worst-case scenario, in which each item was passed on, separately, soon after receipt, and then forgotten, like gossip on the telephone. On this view there could be many transmissions in a short time, and many errors and additions.

If the gospel material did travel like gossip it would surely be influenced by the problems and beliefs of those who passed it on. Items they were not happy with might disappear, or be re-worked

10. Other Approaches

into more acceptable form; though now and then an unwelcome item might get passed on - showing they did not make it up. Thus the gospels report the baptism of Jesus, a little unwillingly, as baptism was for forgiveness of sins, and he was considered sinless. This shows that Jesus really was baptized, as his followers would not have made it up. But we would need more information about the beliefs and practices of those first followers, to make much use of this type of argument.

The comparisons are indeed short, and rounded, and do sometimes misfit their placing in the narrative. If passed on orally, and one by one, some would survive in this locality, some in that; explaining why some ended up in Matthew, and others in Luke, etc. Some which were passed on in public, churchy situations might well undergo deliberate adjustment to the needs and thoughts of their hearers. Perhaps such additions and alterations can be undone, leaving us nearer to the original.

Much work has been done along these lines. It is said, for example, that items originally spoken to 'the crowd' would later get transferred to the disciples, and so be felt to apply to those early Christians who were reading them. To recover the original versions we must re-direct these items to those who first heard them: from disciples to 'crowd'. <u>Burglar,</u> for example, appears in Matthew and Luke as telling church members to stay awake, even though Christ's coming was delayed. Re-directed, this warning applies to everyone: God's Day will come upon you suddenly, dont know when.

4. Editorial activity

If all these scraps of oral tradition came down through many separate individuals, quite major constructive work would have been required to put them together into gospels. In which case the aims and methods of this construction should lie before us, in our gospels. Enquiry into these possibilities is oddly called Redaction Criticism, as it began in the study of minor changes made by one writer when borrowing from another. The term is now applied to any study of how gospels got written, and to backgrounds of debate which might help to explain their special interests.

These various methods of enquiry are not special to the parables, or to Christianity, but form part of many historical enquiries. The questions raised are factual: when we ask what an author originally wrote, or what other books he relied on, and how that information might have

10. Other Approaches

changed on its way to him, these are all matters of historical fact. We may indeed have difficulty in finding the answers, but that does not make those answers depend on our beliefs, hopes, presuppositions etc.

We now turn to consider several modern schools of parable-study. Some of these are factual in intent, seeking to understand the parables as they were first meant to be. Each school also uses certain principles of interpretation, which may not derive from the evidence.

5. Jesus the Jew

Jesus was, surely, a teacher and a Jew. And comparisons were used in teaching, by some rabbis of his time. Did he get this technique from them, ready-made? If so, his stories could be expected to work rather as theirs did; as illustrative parallels. Let us see.

A man angered his son and drove him from home. The man's friend came to plead with him, to let his son return. The father said: Is there anything else you would like to ask concerning my son? For we got reconciled long ago. This is said to explain God saying 'Why do you cry to me? (Exodus 14.15).

155

There is a comparison here. The picture-part is fictional and has no present interest, except to explain something. The reality-part is a passage in Scripture, found obscure.

In his reported parables Jesus does not explain knotty passages of Scripture. He does commend some points already clear but not yet agreed; but spends little time explaining matters already conceded but still found obscure.

Here is another rabbinic parable:
A king invites his servants to join him in a meal. Unsure when to come, some got togged up at once, then just sat around waiting. Others carried on working, expecting to have time to change. Suddenly all are called in, just as they were; some in party dress, others in dirty daytime rig. The king, annoyed, makes the scruffy ones stand and watch the clean ones eat.
So dont put off repenting a sin, for death may catch you unawares.

The point here expounded is a general truth, not a passage from scripture. It is got by making *clean* and *scruffy* stand for sinless and sinner. Other interpretations are waiting to be made.

Stories like these are not much help with the parables of Jesus. Ought we to accept their guidance, because Jesus was a rabbi, and a Jew?

10. Other Approaches

Maybe, if we knew that all rabbis thought and acted like earlier rabbis, never trying anything new. But we dont know this; in fact, we know the opposite.

6. Occasions to match

Some say that each comparison must have been told on some occasion which called it forth. Both parties knew what the occasion was, so they did not mention it. That is why so many parables have reached us occasion-less.

Can we then borrow a peg from elsewhere in the narrative, to provide an occasion for our parable? We know that Jesus recruited volunteers for his cause, so why not take <u>Found Treasure</u> and <u>Found Pearl</u> as telling them how important that was? This procedure is solemnly described as 'setting the parables in the living context of Jesus' Ministry'. Well, it does set them in the context of some suppositions of ours about that Ministry.

7. Surprise, surprise

According to another school, people nowadays cannot honestly accept the time-bound trappings of the gospel message: spirits making humans unwell, choruses of angels, heaven above and hell below. Edit these out, and what is left can still challenge people to a better life.

How Parables Work

Those who favour this 'existentialist' approach pay special attention to certain comparisons which contain details so improbable (they say) that no audience could have swallowed them. How on earth could a slave run up a debt of *ten thousand talents*? How come those dinner-guests *all* developed previous engagements for the same afternoon? Who could credit *four* travellers independently plodding unarmed through well-known bandit country, within an hour of each other? These impossible features must serve some purpose outside of the story. Yes, they were purposely made unbelievable, to smash our everyday complacency, and make us ready for the Word.

Despite our excitement we must ask:
1. Does all true religion consist of authentic personal response to challenges? What about the unchallenged, then?
2. Do really tall stories break people up in bits, all ready for conversion? If so, Science Fiction should have filled our churches up again.

Even granting these points, a question of fact would still remain: (3) were those tales really incredible, making any hearer gag on them?

The picture-part of a spoken comparison does need to be readily understood, and acceptable, so a totally incredible tale would not secure assent to anything. But an unlikely item could be used,

10. Other Approaches

in the context of a Story which made its verdict clear and evident. Those 'impossible' items all came from Stories, not pictures. If we still find them plausible in a Story, then they are not impossible. This wholeAnd the only evidence is of *modern* hearers claiming to find them incredible.

8. Gospellers or novelists

Some have wondered how much of the gospel material could be due to the gospel-writers themselves; not just the expression and arrangement, but the anecdotes and comparisons. Luke in particular has been paid this compliment. He does seem to have written speeches for his characters, to fill out the early years; and he did introduce a whole new section of narrative to accommodate extra comparisons.

Well, did he make up new comparisons? Top Table, perhaps, to suit his idea of a parable. But he also reports several comparisons incomplete; why invent point-less comparisons? And the morals and tips he provides show he had not mastered the form well enough to start composing them.

9. Digging down to basics

Ideas from anthropology have influenced some recent studies of the parables. In any text some *structures* (factors, features, motifs) are due only to the writer, while others reflect his culture and his time; others again belong to humanity at large, everywhere, everywhen. These last *deep structures* structuralists go mining for.

The mining goes like this: (1) shepherd loses sheep, so (2) he'll be in trouble with the boss, indeed (3) he is in a deficiency-situation which urgently needs remedying.

Yes, he surely is, but is that need any deeper and more universal, or is it just a more pompous way of saying the same thing?

Some points in the comparisons are clearly 'cultural' i.e. special and limited to those people and their times; Jewboys would not like herding pigs; a host sees to his dinner first, then summons guests. Not that these time-bound factors make those items impenetrable to us; a commentator can soon help us understand - as you did, just now, by reading this paragraph

The parable-stories, being fictions, are to that extent general; they concern *a* shepherd, *some* king, *any* Pharisee. Structuralists seek generality in their actions: finding lost sheep is a case of recovering what was lost, which in turn exemplifies being better off after being worse. Surely this chain of 'being a case of' will come to an end somewhere; and that is where the 'deep structure' will be found.

10. Other Approaches

Does this logical pastime help us to understand the parables? It does provide one way to classify stories from here, there, and everywhere; thus providing a set of parallels to each comparison. Well, structural-parallels, for much depends who is classifying them.

Who is it, then, that collects these stories, who formulates the deep structures they allegedly exemplify? The anthropologist. who wanted to make anthropological sense of that comparison. He stares defiantly down his cultural telescope, unaware that the patterns he sees may be his eye, reflected back to him.

10. His story or ours

Were you there, asks a popular hymn, when they crucified my lord? No, we weren't, nor you. Nor were we present when he told the people parables, or made them better, or asked the storm to stop. News of these things can now come to us only from written accounts, compiled from word-of-mouth traditions some generations later on, and since re-copied many times on their way to us. We are spectators at a distance, viewing a very remote game, and wondering who puts the right spin on it.

We can still ask what these comparisons mean. Mean to us, now; or meant to them, then? Our study of the parables will be influenced and to some extent determined by our choice between these alternatives. People used to think the only meaning that mattered was what the Teller meant: we may have our own ideas about *Paradise Lost*, but only Milton's ideas can really count, for he created it.

But a book may live on long after the author is dead or even forgotten (*Jonah*, again). So the author's life and society, his acquaintance and reading, the causes he favoured, even his declared intention in writing, all these points on which literary study used to concentrate can no longer determine the meaning of his book. Forget the writer, then, for the meaning is a function of the text.

This sounds like a matter of scholarship: a book has a meaning, which experts can discover and those less expert should accept. On another reading this approach is more revolutionary: the text means whatever each reader takes it to mean. You have an Inalienable Human Right to take the gospels any way you like. So have I. Here the old search for author's meaning may creep in again, for a reader may want to know what the Teller was trying to say, and do, in those parables. If interpretation is entirely free, then they are free to follow this line, and others are not free to tell them not to, not if they espouse the As-You-Like-It approach.

10. Other Approaches

The term polyvalent (many-valued) has muddied this debate. A polyvalent parable may be one carrying several messages. How would this work? Teller and Hearer need one Verdict to agree on, and one Judgment for that Verdict to commend. A Hearer dithering between several Verdicts and multiple Judgments would never get started on the more important bit.

It may be said that <u>Sower</u> was polyvalent, as it had one message for the first Hearers, another for those who first repeated it, and meant something else again to the gospel writer. And for later readers there could be fresh meanings in the tale.

Yes, people have at various times seen different meanings in a parable. Do these all *belong* to the original parable, leaving us free to pick and choose, interpreting it any way we need or want? No. For most hearers, these many meanings are not of equal value or standing. What they mainly want to know about a parable is what the Teller meant by it, and what he hoped to achieve by telling it. The other meanings, as we say dismissively, are of merely 'historical' interest. And that is quite enough about this rather polyvalent term.

11. Verdicts imply Judgments

Besides reviewing approaches with which we partly disagree, we should also salute some earlier scholars who, we think, got it nearly right; noting our debt to them, and asking that their contributions be recognised in our day.

C.H.Dodd has several much-quoted phrases which lean our way: 'the parable is a metaphor or simile drawn from nature or common life, arresting the hearer by its vividness or strangeness, and leaving the mind in sufficient doubt about its precise application to tease it into active thought'
(it) 'presents one single point of comparison'
(it) 'has the character of an argument ... entices the hearer to a judgment on the situation depicted, and challenges him ... to apply that judgment to the matter in hand' (for judgment read Verdict).
and, later 'A parable is a picture or story of real life, presenting a situation which the hearers will recognize ..(and inviting their judgment on it).The judgment .. is to be applied to a different situation present (to their minds.) The characters in the parable (must behave) as such characters might behave in real life. The details ... create dramatic verisimilitude, and rarely have any independent significance'.

10. Other Approaches

For Dodd, what we call the picture-part is everyday, and its Verdict obvious. Each parable has only one Judgment, and both parties knew jolly well what it was.

J. Jeremias follows Dodd but hopes to get closer to the original intention of the parables, finally grouping them under eight themes (here re-phrased):
Salvation is now; God shows mercy; He will win; Bad time coming; Dont miss the bus; Be on lookout; Discipleship pays; With me you can face the Judgment.

Eta Linnemann has a useful discussion of method; what categories were available, and which ones Jesus would have used. She sees parables as a conversational device to win hearers over, with an implicit argument, to get them to change sides. Those sides define the 'situation' which both parties recognised and so do not trouble to state. By offering a story or simile for comparison, and thereby 'claiming one thing for another', the Teller is in a way conceding a point to the other side, who may or may not admit the parallel. If they do admit it, the parable snaps shut, completing an 'interlock' between Teller and Hearers.

On this view the Hearers had to work out what the judgment was; that was all part of the treatment. But someone re-telling the parable later on would need to state the judgment, and indicate in what 'situation' it was enforced. That is why such details are provided in the gospels.

Andrew Parker offers a fuller account of 'two-dimensional speech forms', in which one part reacts with the other; as in satires, riddles, proverbs, coded messages, etc. In some of these one part 'stands for' the other; you talk about the one that comes easier, and leave to your hearer the embarrassment of 'applying' it to the other part. He classes parables with 'illustrations', where A is mentioned with B to say something about B: a boy called up to the beak finds his knees shaking 'like a jelly' (41).

The parables of Jesus, for Parker, offered a form of healing, for overcoming people's 'twisted attitudes'. The relationship in question was first portrayed in some other instance, a harmless, storified picture-part. The hearer might then realise that the twisty bits he was so attached to were similar. This account does not require that Jesus stated his judgment, or that he didnt; but does suggest that the hearers were sometimes sent away so the answer could sink in.

10. Other Approaches

These writers all see parables as forms of persuasion or argument; people needed to get some things straight, and parables were a fairly painless way of achieving this. The views needing correction formed the situation-in-Life for the first telling of the parable, in which both parties knew exactly what that 'situation' was - but later tellers or writers did not know.

Writers who agree how a parable was meant to work may still disagree about what it was meant to achieve; correction, healing, triumph in debate?

12. A conclusion

This chapter has set out several approaches to the parables which I find inappropriate, and another which is welcomed in this book. The reader, having inspected them all, must decide for himself.

Our findings in earlier chapters were summarized as we went along. Here we repeat the firmest points - if only to show where the guessing has to start.

Most gospel parables include interactive features, to engage the Hearers' attention and support. These are found in all the lines of tradition, and are stable across those lines: features found in one report also turn up in parallel reports. These features have no part to play in a written account, so belong further back. The Teller needed his Hearers to agree his Verdict for the picture-part, to give him a lever for enforcing the parallel Judgment.

Some parables are reported with a Judgment. Others end with the Verdict. In both cases the judgment was to be enforced by parity of reasoning from the Verdict, to which the Judgment would be 'parallel'. Maybe in these cases the Hearers were not told what the judgment was, as they already knew; or maybe those judgments were all stated, like the rest, but some then got lost. Either way, these 'missing' Judgments have given rise to the great mass of speculative interpretation of the parables; to which we added just a mite.

The gospel-writers were aware that some of their parable-reports were defective, and did what they could to remedy these defects. They were largely unsuccessful in this, but their efforts did show that neither they nor a previous 'creative community' could have been responsible for the substance or form of those parables.

Where a judgment is missing we shall have to guess at it, if we want to make sense of that parable. Here are some suggestions on how to guess:

10. Other Approaches

1. First, study the picture-part on its own, and express in a Verdict what that picture-part sought agreement to.
2. Glance cautiously at any morals pegs or groupings.
3. Consider only those judgments that match the Verdict so closely as to convince a Hearer that he couldnt dodge it any longer.

NOTES to Chapter Ten

<u>New Testament scholarship</u> (1) some reviews:
Foster *Four for the Gospel Makers*
Palmer *Logic of Gospel Criticism*
Schweitzer *Quest of the Historical Jesus* (for C19)
Barton *Camb Companion to Bib Interpretation*, 9f.

<u>Gospel headings</u>. (2)
Metzger *The New Testament: .. Growth* , 96

<u>Dating</u> (2)
Gallio was proconsul in Greece about 50-52 AD;
Pilate was procurator of Judaea 26-36.
Fuller *Critical Introduction to N Testament* , 11
Grant *Historical Intro to the New Testament*, 432

<u>Borrowing</u> (2): still under debate
Lowe "... arguments, order to Markan priority"
Calvert "... criteria for ... words of Jesus"
Sanders "Argument from Order..."

<u>Approaches to the parables</u> (4)
See Parker *Painfully Clear* 10, and
Gillingham "Parables as attitude change"
Bailey & Broek *Literary Forms in NT*
Westermann *Parables of Jesus* 153;
Bultmann *History of the Synoptic Tradition* 166

10. Other Approaches

<u>Rabbinic parables</u> (5)
Jones *Art & Truth* 66.
Bowker *Targums and Rabbinic Literature*, 102f.
Flusser *Die Rabbinische Gleichnisse* 23f.
Young *Jesus and his Jewish Parables*.

<u>'Impossible' features</u> (7), noticed in:
<u>Mean Debtor</u>*, <u>Missing Guests</u>, and <u>Good Samaritan</u>* and even in <u>Weeds</u> and <u>Prodigal</u> (Jones *Art & Truth,* 37).
See also Beavis *Power of Jesus Parables*.

<u>Structuralist approach</u> (9)
Patte *What is Structural Exegesis*, 4.
Thurber *Carnival,* 257 'youve drawn your eye'

<u>Verdicts imply Judgments</u> (11)
C.H.Dodd *Parables of the Kingdom,* 16,18,23
Interpretation of Fourth Gospel, 134
A.T.Cadoux *P of Jesus their art and use,* 13,45
J.Jeremias *Parables of Jesus,* 9,115
E.Linnemann *Parables of Jesus,* 24, 27
A.Parker *Painfully Clear,* 65 - 71

Chapter Eleven

The Gospel Comparisons

THESE TRANSLATIONS attempt a story-teller's style. Mark's come first, then Matthew's, then Luke's. They are based, by kind permission, on a text of the New Testament published by the Bible Society.

above a comparison comes its <u>name,</u> with
reference on the left, and peg if any.
parallels on the right, by chapters:
and a para-number from *Gospel Parallels*.

below the comparison comes its *Verdict,* and then
its JUDGMENT, in small caps if given,
in plain print if suggested,
<in brackets, if a guess>;
with a coding of its main features (see 230)

MARK

2.15 bad company?   <u>dont need doctor</u>   M9, L5 : 53

      He was having a meal at home. Many tax-folk and sinners were there, sitting down along with Jesus and his disciples; all were part of his company. When the scribes saw him eating with sinners and taxmen, they quizzed his disciples: now he's eating with taxmen and sinners? Jesus heard, and gave this reply: Its the sick who need doctors, not those who are fit. And its the sinners I came to help.

   only the sick need doctoring
   Only sinners need helping to repent   PAJ.TR

2.18 fasting   <u>fast</u> <u>later</u>   M9, L5 : 54

      John's disciples and the Pharisees were on a fast. So Jesus was asked How come your folk aren't fasting, when John's people are, and the Pharisees? Jesus replied The bridegroom's party cannot fast, not while he is with them. Later on, when he's gone, then they will fast.

     groomsmen dont fast
     Why should we?   PAO.TR

2.21   spoilt coat+ bottles   M9, L5:54

Nobody's going to patch an old coat with unbleached cloth, for the new bit would pull at the old, and make the tear even worse. And no-one puts new wine in old bottles, for they would burst, losing the wine and spoiling the bottle as well. No, new wine must go into new bottles.

  mending / re-use makes worse
  <no good patching our old government>   PWO.XZ/1C

3.22 devil's help   divide and ruin   M2, L11: 86

The scribes from Jerusalem said He is possessed. Driving out devils, is he? Their Prince must be helping him! Jesus called the people together and replied in a comparison: How can Satan expel Satan? A kingdom torn by civil war cannot survive, nor can a family. Satan would really be done for, if he took up arms against himself. If the devil is in rebellion against himself, that's the end of him.

  division weakens, fatally
  SATAN DIVIDED IS SATAN FINISHED   PWJ.TR/kClmE

3.27   first subdue   M12,L11: 86

   You cant just walk in to a tough guy's place and rip off his stuff. You've got to tie him up first. Then you really can shift the goods.

  first tie up householder
  <Satan is tied up now>   PWO.X

11. Gospel Comparisons – Mark

4.2 parables   <u>Sower</u>   M13,L8 : 90

    Much of his teaching was in comparisons. Listen here. This farmer went out sowing seed. Some of the seed fell on the road: along came the birds and ate it up. Some fell on shallow stony patches, and soon sprang up: up comes the sun and scorches it; with no root it just withered away. Some seeds fell among thistles, which grew up and throttled them. No yield there. But some of the seed fell on good ground; it grew up and swelled and gave a crop thirty, sixty, even a hundred times what was sown. Now use your ears.   (An explanation: 4.13)

    Some seed lost, but harvest great.
    <that goes for preaching too>   SOE.TC

4.21   <u>lamp</u>   M5, L8 : 94

    People dont bring a lamp to stick under the bed, do they, or under a bucket? They set it up on the lampstand. And why do people hide things? Only so they can find them again. What is hidden is there to be revealed. If you can hear me, you listen good.

    lights are to see by
    <so are parables>   PAO.D/mB

How Parables Work

4.26 God's rule   <u>seed</u>   : 95

This chap sowed seed on his field. And he was sleeping at home, up and about in the day. Meanwhile that seed sprang up and grew, but he never knew a thing about it. The earth bears its fruit on its own, stalk first, then ear, and finally corn. And when the crop is ready, he's in at once with his sickle, for harvest has come. That's what God's rule is like.

> *growth unseen, harvest obvious*
> when kingdom comes, you'll know   POH.D

4.30   mustard   M13, L8 : 97

About God's rule. Just think of a mustard seed. When sown it is tinier than other seeds, but it grows up higher than them, with great big branches, so even birds can shelter in its shade.

> *tiny seed big bush*
> kingdom could grow like that   POH.D/kmC

7.14 dirty hands   <u>food and dirt</u>   M15 : 115

Nothing coming into a man from outside can dirty him, but only what comes out. At home his disciples asked him to explain. You really are thick, he said. Cant you see that what comes in from outside cant make you dirty, as it goes into the tummy (not the heart}, and down into the drain (this remark made all foods 'clean'). Its what comes out that dirties you. Evil thoughts come out from the heart: so do wrong sex, stealing, murder, adultery, coveting, wickedness; deceit and lust, not to mention

11. Gospel Comparisons – Mark

envy, slander, pride, and other foolishness. All these bad things come from inside, and make you unclean. (This saying made all foods clean.)

    its what comes out that dirties you
        <bad thoughts are dirtier>   PWJE.QTC

9.50 offences   salt   M5,L14   :132

Salt is fine, while it keeps its taste. Once that goes, nothing can bring it back. Have salt among yourselves and be at peace with each other.

    Cant revive stale salt
        < X, once gone, is gone for good >   POUY.D/kJ

12.1 by what right?   Tenants Kill   M21,L20:204

This chap planted a vineyard, fenced it, dug a well and built a tower, then let it off to tenants. Come harvest he sent a man for his share of the crop, but they beat him and sent him off empty-handed. Another man was sent but he got thumped disgracefully. The next one was killed; and many others who went were flayed or done to death. The owner had only one left, his favourite son, so he sent him last of all, thinking 'surely they will respect my son'. Those tenants thought otherwise: 'here is the heir' they said, 'come on, let's kill him and we can keep the land'. So they killed him and threw his body out of the vineyard. So what is the owner going to do? He will come and destroy those tenants, and re-let the vineyard to others.

    Owner will punish them and re-let
        <this government has had it >   SVAO.TC

13.28 His day   <u>signs of end</u>   M24, L21:22

    Learn this lesson from the fig. When its branches are supple and the leaves come out then you know summer is just round the corner. And when these things start happening you will know that Day is very near.

       fig shows summer coming
       THESE EVENTS SHOW END IS NEAR   PJU.CD

13.33 dont know when   <u>doorman</u>   :222

    Watch out, keep awake, for you never know when It'll happen. Remember that chap who left home telling each man to carry on with his job; and the doorman was just told to keep awake, as you never know when the boss will turn up, late on maybe, or at midnight, or cockcrow, or even crack of dawn. And if he did turn up all of a sudden he might catch you fast asleep. You - and everyone- have just got to keep awake.

       waiting up is his job
       AND YOURS   PJU.D

MATTHEW

5.13 sermon   <u>salt</u>   K9, L14 : 20

You are the salt of the earth. But salt that's gone off cannot be re-saltified. It is no good for anything. You just chuck it out, and people tread it in.

         cant re-saltify
     <some X is done for, once it's stale>   POUY.D/kJ

5.14   <u>lamp</u>   K4, L8 : 20

You are this world's light. A village on a hill cannot be hidden; and a lamp when lit is never stuck under a bucket, but set on a lampstand to give light to everyone in the house. And your light must shine out so people see the good you do and give glory to your father in heaven.

         lights are to see by
         GOOD DEEDS SHOW THE WAY   PAO.D/mB

5.25   <u>last farthing</u>   L12 : 22

Try to be pleasant and make it up with your opponent, while on your way to court. Otherwise he'll drag you off to the judge, who'll pass you on to the sergeant, and you'll end up in jail. You'll have to pay up the very last penny, I can tell you, before you can get out.

         settle out of court
            ? non-comparison   PYO.TN/mD

How Parables Work

6.22   e<u>y</u>e<u>lights</u>   L11 : 33

The eye lights up the body. With a clear eye the whole body is lit up, but with a bad eye all is in the dark. If your light turns to darkness, how dark that will be.

         it's all you have to see with
         <your X is irreplaceable>   PWAOU.D.lT

6.24   <u>two bosses</u>   L16 : 34

Work for two bosses? Its impossible! You'll either hate A and favour B, or despise B and hold by A. You cant serve God *and* Money.

         can't serve both
         NOT GOD *AND* MONEY   PWAJU.D

7.3   <u>log in eye</u>   L 6 : 36

Why stare at that little smut in your brother's eye, never noticing the plank in your own? How can you offer to take out his little smut, when all the time yours has that girt big plank in. Take the plank out first, you twerp, then you'll see properly to remove his smut.

         get your own eyes seen to first
         <and your morality>   PWAOU.D

11. Gospel Comparisons – Matthew

7.6   pig food   : 37

Dont give something holy to the dogs, or throw your pearls down in front of pigs, for they'll tread them into the mud, turn around, and tear into you.

        disappointed and enraged
        <mind whom you preach to >   POU.D

7.7 asking for things   snake sandwich   L11 : 38

Suppose your boy was asking for bread, would you give him a stone? Or a snake, in place of fish? Rotters you may be, but you do know what's good for your own kids. And so does your father in heaven, he's quite sure to give good things to those who ask.

        won't give your kid one
        God's an even better giver   PWJUE.D

7.15 go by deeds   trees and fruit   L6 : 41

Look out for those phoney preachers who come togged up as sheep. Sheep indeed! Its wolves they are, all ready to snatch and tear. Their 'fruits' will show them up. People dont pick figs from thistles, do they, or harvest grapes from brambles? A good tree bears good fruit, a bad one carries bad. A good tree just cant carry bad fruit, nor a bad tree good. Any tree not bearing good fruit gets chopped down and burnt. It's the fruits you tell them by.

        good tree , good fruit
        judge people by what they *do*   PWJU.D/1O

7.24   two builders   L 6 : 43

Someone who hears my teaching and then goes and does it is like that chap who dug down to the rock, when building his house. Down came the rains, up came the floods and spread abroad, the winds raged and blew and that house took a real battering, but it never fell, for it was built upon the rock. But that other silly chap built slap upon the sand. Down came the rains, up welled the floods, along blew the winds, they all smashed against that house, and down it came. My, what a crash! And that sort of crash is waiting for anyone who doesnt do what I say.

>   *well built, flood-proof*
>   better do what I say   PBH.D

9.10 bad company   dont need doctor   K2, L5 : 53

Jesus was taking his meal at home, and lots of taxmen and wrongdoers came and sat to eat with him. Seeing this the Pharisees quizzed his disciples Why does your teacher sit and eat with taxmen and sinners? Jesus heard it and replied Its the sick who need doctors, not those who are fit. And its sinners I came to call, not the good people. You need a lesson on that saying, 'Its mercy I want, not sacrifice'. I came to call sinners, not the other lot.

>   *only the sick need doctoring*
>   ITS SINNERS THAT NEED HELPING TO REPENT   PAJ.TR

11. Gospel Comparisons – Matthew

9.14 fasting   <u>fast later</u>   K2 L5 : 54

John's disciples came and asked How is it we are fasting, like the Pharisees, but your people arent? Well, said Jesus, did you ever hear of a bridegroom's party having a good weep? Will they go into mourning? Not while he's there they wont. Later on, after he's gone, that's when they'll fast.

    groomsmen dont mourn
    so why should we fast?   PAO.TR

9.16   <u>spoilt coat & bottles</u>   K2 L5 : 54

Who's going to patch an old coat with unbleached cloth? The patch would pull at the coat, making the tear even worse. Whoever will store new wine in old bottles? They'd burst, smashing the bottles and losing all the wine. No, new wine needs new bottles, then both are safe.

  patching worsens; old bottles burst
 <no good patching our old government>   PWO.XZ/1C

9.37 preaching mission   <u>send more men</u>   L10 : 58

We have a great harvest, but not enough men to gather it! Better ask the boss to put more workers on the job.

    need more harvesters
    only God supplies preachers   POEU.D

How Parables Work

11.16 John baptist asks   <u>kids at play</u>   L7 : 65
People nowadays? They're like children sitting in the market-place and shouting to their friends,
    We did the piping bit but you never danced,
    Not even a tear though we did sing the lament.
Look you now, John came, no drink, no food, so people said The devil's got into him. Then along comes the Son of man, enjoying his meals, and they say What a glutton, a wino, palling up with taxmen and sinners! And is God's wisdom in the right? The proof lies in what he does.
       cant agree what to play
       you lot are never satisfied   PJHF.T

12.11 Sabbath healing?   <u>Your ox</u>   L6 : 70
This chap whose hand was all dried up was there in synagogue. They put it to Jesus, Is it O K to heal on Sabbath? He said If one of you had just one ox, and it got stuck in the mud on Sabbath, wont he get a rope and pull him out? And a man is worth much more than an ox. So doing good on Sabbath is allowed.
    You rescue on Sabbath
    doing good on sabbath is OK   PWBUY.TR/1E

11. Gospel Comparisons – Matthew

12.24 devil's help   <u>divide and ruin</u>   K3, L11 : 86
The Pharisees said, if he does cast out devils, it must be with their prince's help. Jesus could see what they were getting at. A kingdom will lose its people, he said, if torn by civil war, and a house or a city divided will not survive. Now if Satan is casting out Satan, that is civil war, and his kingdom is finished. And if Satan is helping me then whose help are your people getting, in that job? So your own folk will be condemning you. But if its by God's help I am healing, then his kingdom has caught up with you.
  division weakens, fatally
 Satan divided is Satan finished PWJ.XR/kClmE

12.29   <u>first subdue</u>   K3, L11 : 86
You cant just walk in to a tough guy's house and plunder his goods. You'ld have to tie him up first. Only then you can shift his stuff.
  first tie up householder
  Satan is tied up now PWO.X

12.33   <u>trees and fruits</u> (2) :86, see 7.16
If the tree is good then its fruit will be good as well; and bad trees carry bad fruit. For the tree is known by its fruit. Come on, viperlets, why is it you cant say anything good? Its because you're bad. You're full to bursting with it, and then it all comes out.
  good tree , good fruit
 <bad people cant say good things> PWJU.D/lO

12.35   <u>two shopmen</u>   L 6 : 86

A good trader brings out good stuff, for his shop is well-stocked; and what can the low fellow next door drag out from his junk-hole? Junk, of course!

> *good trader, sound goods*
> *for good deeds, you need good thoughts*   POE

12.39 a sign, please   <u>men of nin + Q of south</u>   L11 : 87

Scribes and Pharisees were demanding a sign. Look you, he said, the folk of today are a rotten misbehaved lot, always scratching around for a sign. Here's Jonah's, then - and that's all you'll get. He was inside that fish three days and nights, just as the Son of man will be, down in the earth. And when Judgment Day comes the men of Nineveh will lead the case against you, for they did repent at Jonah's message; and someone greater than Jonah is with you now. And the Queen of the South will testify too, for she came from the ends of the earth to hear Solomon's wisdom; and someone greater than Solomon is with you now.

> *repented when called /*
> *came far to hear Solomon*
> *but you lot didn't*   PJU.TZ/mXR

12.43   <u>Vacant Possession</u>   L11: 88

When that dirty devil comes out of a man it goes through dry and dusty places but finds nowhere to stay. Hold on, it

11. Gospel Comparisons – Matthew

says, why not go back to that house I was in. Back it goes, and finds the house empty, swept clean and all put straight. Off he goes again, rounding up seven other devils, even worse, and they all come in and squat. So that man is even worse off than he was before. Now you know what is coming to you.

    tenants bad, squatters worse
        non-comparison?   SJY.N/1O

13.3 parables   <u>Sower</u>   K4, L8 : 90

(Much of his teaching was in comparisons.) Listen here. This farmer went out sowing his seed. Some of it fell on the road, but the birds came along and ate it up. Some fell on shallow stony patches, and soon sprang up, and got scorched by the sun and withered quite away, for it had no root. Some fell among thistles, which grew up and throttled it. No yield there. But some of the seed fell on good ground, and their crop was a hundred or sixty or thirty times what was sown. Now use your ears.

                (13.18 explains)
    Some seed lost, but harvest great.
    same goes for preaching too   SOE.TC

13.24   <u>Weeds</u>   : 96

This man had good seed sown in his field. But an enemy came by night and sowed weeds over it, and went off. The seed sprouted and began to grow, and the weeds came up alongside. They reported it: Sir, wasnt that good seed you had sown in your field? Where did the weeds come from?

How Parables Work

Some enemy must be at work, he said. Should we go, then, and gather up the weeds? No, you might uproot corn as well. Let both grow on until harvest. I'll tell the reapers to gather up weeds first in bundles to burn, then to bring the corn into my barn. And that's what God's rule is like.

            (13.36 explains)

 weeding must wait for harvest
 judgment will come - at the end   SOHE.DC

13.31   <u>mustard</u>   K4, L8 : 97

Another comparison. This chap sowed mustard in his field. It's one of the tiniest of seeds, but it grows up bigger than other plants, almost a tree; birds come and nest in its branches. That what God's rule is like.

 tiny seed big bush
 kingdom could grow like that   POH.D/kmC

13.33   <u>yeast</u>   L13 : 98

God's kingdom? Well, it's like when a woman took yeast and mixed it into three measures of wheat flour, until all of it was leavened.

 leavens the lot
 kingdom pervasive   PWOH.D/mC

13.44   <u>found treasure + found pearl</u>   : 101

This treasure lay buried in a field. One chap found it, re-buried it, and went off – over the moon - to sell everything he had and buy that field. Or think of a pearl-merchant,

11. Gospel Comparisons – Matthew

who found one that was absolutely superb, sold all he had and bought it. That's how it is with the kingdom.

> *sold all, to buy*
> kingdom worth everything   POH.DZ

13.47   <u>sorting fish</u>   : 102

This fishing-net was cast into the sea, and all sorts of fish came into the net. When full, they brought it ashore, sat down, collected the good ones into jars, and chucked out the rubbish. So too, at the Worlds End, angels will be out on patrol to sort out the baddies and throw them in the fire. There'll be wailing then, and shivering with fear. And that's how God's kingdom will be.

> *rubbish gets chucked out*
> RUBBISH-PEOPLE TOO   PJH.D

13.51   <u>new and old</u>   :103

Did you take that all in? Yes, we did. Which shows you that a scribe schooled in the kingdom is like a householder who brings out new things and old from his storecupboard.

> *prudent householder uses both*
> kingdom- scribe will offer both   POH.D

15.10 dirty hands   <u>food and dirt</u>   K7 : 115

Calling the crowd back he said Now listen, and think: What goes into your mouth doesn't dirty you, it's what comes out. That is what makes people unclean. His disciples came and told him, you realise the Pharisees heard this, and took offence? Well, he said, every plant God didnt sow will get pulled up. Never mind them, they are 'blind leaders'; and if one blind man leads another both will end up in the bog. Peter then asked him to explain the parable. Well, you really are thick! Cant you see that what comes in at the mouth goes on to the tummy and out into the drain. But what comes out of the mouth is from the heart; and that's what dirties a man. Out come his evil thoughts: murder, prostitution, adultery, theft, false witness and slander. These are what make people dirty. Eating without washing the hands wont dirty anyone.

    what comes out dirties you
    bad thoughts are dirtier   PWJE.QTC

[The next two come in <u>food and dirt,</u> but can be taken on their own.]

13.13 <u>God's garden</u>   : 103
anything growing there which He didnt plant is going to get pulled up.

    that's farming
    <it works here too>   PO.D

15.14 <u>blind leader</u>   L6 : 115
Can one blind man guide another? Wouldnt both end up in the mud?

    cant see where they're going
    <no more our leaders can>   PWAO.D/1C

11. Gospel Comparisons – Matthew

16.2 sign please 2   <u>signs of times</u>   L12 : 160

Both Pharisees and Sadducees came demanding a sign from above, to put him on the spot. He replied, Of an evening you say It will be fine tomorrow, for the sky is red. And next morning, There'll be a storm today, look at that horrible red sky. How is it you can predict weather, but cant read the signs of the times?

    you forecast weather
    WHY NOT EVENTS?   PU.X/1T

18.12 dont despise   <u>Lost Sheep</u>   L 15 : 133

Now you tell me: if a chap had a hundred sheep to look after, and one went astray, wont he leave the others there on the fells and go off hunting for the missing one? And let me tell you this: if he does find that one he'll make more fuss over it than over the ninety-nine who never went astray. For your father in heaven does not want to lose any of our little ones.

    so glad he found it
    GOD KEEN NOT TO LOSE ANY   SWAJ.DZ/1XC

18.21 Peter's question   <u>Mean Debtor</u>   :136

Peter asked How many times do I have to let my brother off when he keeps on doing the dirty on me? Would seven times be enough? No, said Jesus, more like seventy times seven. It's like that king who decided to check his servants' accounts. Right at the start one was brought in who owed him a hundred thousand pounds, which he couldn't possibly repay. So the boss gave orders for him to be sold, with his wife and children and all his possessions, towards the debt. The servant got down and begged: Give me time and I will pay it all. So the boss felt sorry for him and set him free, and even let him off the debt. Going out he bumped into another servant, who owed him a pound; grabbed him and started throttling him, shouting Pay me what you owe. So that man got down and pleaded, Give me time, I will repay. But he wouldnt have it. Off he went and had him put in jail until he paid back all of it. The other servants were very upset to see what had happened, and they went and told the boss. He called the first man back; You wicked servant, I let you off all that debt, because you begged me to. Shouldnt you take pity on your fellow-servant, as I did on you? And in a rage he handed him over to the torturers, until he paid the lot. Which is what my heavenly father will do to you, unless each of you forgives his brother quite sincerely.

do as you were done by
Or else!   SBHEU.D

20.1 disciples' reward   <u>Half-Day Work</u>   : 190
This chap went out early to hire workers, and agreed with them for a pound a day; and sent them off to his vineyard. About mid-morning he found others standing around in the marketplace, unemployed, and took them on saying You also go to the vineyard, and I will pay you a fair rate.

11. Gospel Comparisons – Matthew

So they went. The same happened again at midday and mid-afternoon. And going out again late on he found others standing there. Why do you stand there all day long, he asked, doing nothing? Because no-one took us on, they said. So he said You also go along to the vineyard. Now when evening came the boss told his steward to call the men and pay them all, last in first out. Those taken on last got a pound. Those employed earlier got the same, but expected more. They started grousing at the boss, We did all the hard work, in the heat of the day, but these fellows only worked one hour. Now you've paid them both the same! He took one aside and said My friend, I'm not cheating you. You agreed for one pound. Here it is. Take your wages and go home. If I want to pay others the same as you, well, its my money, isnt it? Or is it my generosity that makes you jealous? Another tale of the kingdom, showing how the last come first and the first come last.

> *overpaying Peter is no loss to Paul*
> all enter kingdom on same terms SOHF.T

21.28 by what right?   Two Sons   : 203
Answer me this one. A man had two sons. He went to the older one and said My boy, please go and work in the vineyard today. Shant, said the boy; but thought better of it afterwards, and went. The father also asked the younger boy. Yes Sir, he said; but he never went. Now which of them did what the father wanted? The first, they said. Yes, said Jesus. And I can tell you that the taxmen and

prostitutes will get into the kingdom ahead of you. For John came on the orthodox side and they accepted his message, but you didnt. Even after seeing their response you still didnt change your mind.

> *Shant* did *as told, thats what counts*
> Do you?   SVAJUY.XR

21.33   <u>Tenants Kill</u>   K12, L20 : 204

 Another parable. This landowner had a vineyard planted up, fenced, and a well dug, and a tower put up for security. Then he let it off to tenants, and went away. And at harvest-time he sent his men to bring his share of the crop, but the tenants beat them up, killing some and stoning others. He sent others, more of them, but they got the same treatment. Later on he sent his son, thinking 'surely they will respect my boy'. But those tenants thought otherwise: 'here is the heir, come on, let's kill him and we can keep the land'. So they took him and threw him out of the vineyard, and killed him. Now, when the boss comes, what will he do to those tenants? They say, He will destroy them completely, and re-let the vineyard to others who will give him the crop, when harvest comes. And Jesus said to them Did you not read in the Scriptures that 'The stone which was no use to the builders is now the head of the corner, it is God's doing, and a miracle for us.' That's why I say that God's kingdom will be taken away from you and given to another nation, who bear the fruits required.

11. Gospel Comparisons – Matthew

owner will punish them and re-let
FOREIGNERS WILL DESERVE THE KINGDOM   SVAO.TC

22.1   Missing Guests   L14 : 205

(Another comparison for the kingdom.) This king had a wedding party for his son. He sent his men to call the guests, but they didn't want to come. Other men were sent to say: My dinner is all ready, the bulls and fatted cattle are killed, everything is prepared. Please come to the wedding. But the guests took no notice, and went about their own affairs: one to his farm, another to his wholesale business. Some even got hold of those servants and beat them up or killed them. So the king got mad, and sent his army to destroy those murderers and burn down their town. Then he said to his men, The feast is ready but those guests were not fit. You go out into the byways and invite everyone you find there. So they went out and rounded up everyone they found there, bad as well as good. That filled the dining hall. The king came in to review his new guests, and saw one who had not put on the wedding rig. My friend, he said, why did you come in here without the wedding garment? No reply. Then the king told his men to tie him up hand and foot and chuck him out in the dark, where people groan and shiver with fear. For many are invited but only a few will get chosen.

No-shows replaced by will-comes
Same goes for kingdom-feast   SO.X/lR

24.32 Son of man's day   signs of end   K13, L21 : 220

How Parables Work

Learn this lesson from the fig. When its branches are supple and the leaves come out you know that summer is close at hand. And when you actually see these things happening, you will know that Day is very near. They are all going to happen, in your lifetime or mine.

fig shows summer coming
THESE EVENTS SHOW END IS NEAR   PJU.D

24.37   <u>noah's day</u>   L17 : 224

The Son of man's return will be like old Noah's day; people just carried on, eating, drinking, getting married, until the day Noah went aboard the boat; and didnt realise even then, until the flood hit them, and killed the lot.

never saw flood coming
caught out on big day   PBJ.DZ

24.42   <u>burglar</u>   L12 : 225

If the man had known when the burglar would come, he'd have stayed up to stop him breaking in. You too be ready, for the Son of man will turn up unexpectedly.

dont know when to expect
GOT TO BE READY FOR SON OF MAN   PWAJUY.D/1C

24.45   <u>Two Stewards</u>   L12 : 226

Think of a faithful and sensible servant put in charge of the others, to give out their rations; he'll do well if the boss finds things so when he returns. He'll put him in charge of everything! But a bad servant in his place might think 'The boss is taking his time', and start thumping the

11. Gospel Comparisons – Matthew

others, feasting and boozing with the drunkards. And his boss will turn up unexpectedly, carve him up and chuck him out, to join the moaners and groaners outside.

    boss will come and sort them out
    <so will God>   SWYO.D

25.1   Ten Girls   : 227

Ten lasses with lamps were to welcome the bridegroom to his wedding; five sensible, and five others who came with no spare oil. The bridegroom was delayed, and all ten nodded off. At midnight a shout went up The bridegroom's here, go out to meet him. So they all woke up and trimmed their lamps. Now the sillies start begging, Please spare us a bit of oil, our lamps are going out. No, there's not enough for both. Go to the oil shop and fill up there. Which they did. And the bridegroom arrived. So those who were ready went in with him to the feast, and the door was locked. The others came afterwards, shouting Sir, Sir, let us in! Certainly not, I dont know who you are! So keep awake, you dont know when It will be.

    too late really is too late
    YOU'VE GOT TO BE READY, IT WONT WAIT   SOHF.D

25.14   Your Money Back   L19 : 228

This chap was going abroad. He called his personal servants and handed over his money to them, five hundred pounds to one, two hundred to another, one hundred to a third, depending on their skill in business. Then he set off. The first man started trade at once, and doubled his money. So did the second. But the third man dug a hole in the ground, and hid his hundred there. After a long absence the boss came back, and held a reckoning. The first man came and said Sir you gave me five hundred and I've made as much again. There's a fine fellow, said the boss, you're in line for promotion. Come and join in the party. Mr Two-hundred also said he'd doubled it, and had the same welcome from the boss. Then comes the third man: Sir I knew you for a tough one, harvesting next-door's field and gathering sheaves you'd never sown. That scared me. So I hid your money in the ground. Here, take it back, it's all yours. You rotten ditherer, said the boss. You knew I harvest next-door's field, did you, and gather sheaves I'd never sown? Well then, you should have given my money to the bankers. They would have paid it back with interest. Take that hundred off him and give it to five-hundred man! Havers keep getting, almost too much, while the have-not loses his little tiny bit. And chuck that useless servant out to join the moaners and groaners in the darkness outside.

Dont bury investments
<what about Gods gift to you?>   SYOEF.T/lC

11. Gospel Comparisons – Matthew

25.31   Sheep and Goats   :   :229

When the Son of man and all his angels make their glorious re-entry, he will take his seat on that impressive throne, to give judgment on all the people of the earth, sorting them out as a shepherd sorts his flock, sheep on the right and goats to the left. And to those on his right the king will say, You have my father's blessing, come take up the kingdom waiting for you ever since the world was made. For you fed me when I was hungry, gave me a drink when thirsty, as a stranger you took me in, helped me out when I had nothing to wear, looked after me when ill, and visited me in prison. Then these good people will reply Lord, when did we see you hungry or thirsty, and gave you food or drink? When did we take you in as a stranger, or clothe you when short, or visit you in sickness or in prison? And the king will tell them If you did it to any little fellow in the brotherhood, you did it to me.

Then he will say to those on his left, On your way, curse you, to hell you go, the fire's already stoked up for the devil and his messengers. You didnt feed me when hungry, and when I was thirsty you never gave me a drink. You never took me in as a stranger, or gave me clothing when I was without; if I was sick and in prison you did not look after me. And these also will answer back, Sir when did we see you hungry, thirsty, a stranger, short of clothing, ill or in prison, and failed to look after you? If you failed one of them, he said, however junior, then you failed me. So these folk will go off to eternal punishment, but the good will go on to life eternal.

> *its what you do that counts*
>   [not a comparison]   SOU.DN

LUKE

5.30 bad company   <u>dont need doctor</u>   K2, M9 : 53

The scribes and Pharisees were grousing at his disciples, Why do you eat with taxmen and sinners? Jesus replied Its the sick who need doctors, not those who are fit. I came to ask sinners to repent, not the good people.

> *only the sick need doctoring*
> ONLY SINNERS NEED HELPING TO REPENT   PAJ.TR

5.33 fasting   <u>fast later</u>   K2, M9 : 54

They told him, John's disciples are always fasting and praying. So are the Pharisees. But your lot are feasting and boozing. Jesus replied The bridegroom's party cant fast, can they, not while he is with them? Later on, after he's gone, that's when they'll fast.

> *groomsmen dont fast*
> *why should we?*   PAO.TR

5.36   <u>spoilt coat & bottles</u>   K2,M9 : 54

And he gave them a comparison: No-one is going to cut up a new coat, to patch an old one with, for that would leave him with one new coat (with a hole in) plus an old coat (with a mismatched patch). And no-one stores new wine in old bottles, for they would burst, and then he'd have lots of unusable bottles, and wine all over the floor. No, new wine needs new bottles. And no-one will ask for new when he's drinking old; Its good stuff this, he says.

    patching worsens; old bottles burst
    no good patching this old government   PWO.XZ/1C

6.39 sermon   <u>blind leader</u>   M15 : 76

Another comparison. Can one blind man guide another? Wont both end up in the mud?

    cant see where theyre going
    <no more our leaders can>   PWAO.D/1C

6.41   <u>log in eye</u>   M7 : 76

Why stare at a little smut in your brother's eye, when you've got a great big plank in your own? How on earth can you offer to take out his smut, when you cant even see your plank? Take that plank out first, you twerp, then you'll see properly to remove his smut.

    get your own eyes seen to first
    <and your morality>   PWAOU.D

6.43   <u>trees and fruit</u>   M7 : 77

A good tree cant bear bad fruit, nor a bad tree good. Each tree is known by its fruit. People dont pick figs from thistles, do they, nor harvest grapes from brambles?

    good tree, good fruit
    <judge people by what they do >   PWJU.D/1O

11. Gospel Comparisons – Luke

6.45   <u>two shopmen</u>   M13 : 77

This good chap brings out decent stuff from his well-stocked warehouse, but the low fellow next-door puts out junk, it's all he has. (His heart is so full, it all comes out in what he says.)

     good stock, sound goods
     only good people can say good things   POE.D

6.47   <u>two builders</u>   M7 : 78

One chap comes to hear me and then does what I said. He's like a man who dug deep down to the rock to make a foundation for his house; and when a flood came the stream dashed against that house but it never budged, because it was solidly built. Another fellow does hear me, but doesnt do what I said. He's like a man who built slap upon the sand, with no foundation at all; the stream dashed against it and it just came down. My, what a smash-up that was!

     well-built, flood-proof
     better do what I say   PBH.D

7.31 John baptist asks   <u>kids at play</u>   M11 : 82

You people nowadays, you're just like children sitting in the square and calling across to their mates,

     You never danced, though we piped for you,
     we sang the lament but you couldnt even cry.

How Parables Work

For John Baptist came fasting, and you said The devil's got into him. Then comes the Son of man, eating and drinking, and you say Look what a glutton, a wino, palling up with taxmen and sinners! But Wisdom's 'children' always show her in the right.

        cant agree what to play
        you lot are never satisfied   PJHF.T

7.40 dining out   <u>two debtors</u>   : 83

  Dining at Simon's, Jesus puts a point to him. There were two people owing t the same money-lender; five pounds the one, and the other five hundred. Neither could pay him back. So he let them both off. Which will be the gratefuller? The one who owed more, I suppose, said Simon. That's right. And you see this woman? When I came in you didnt give water to wash the feet, but she keeps on wetting them with tears and using her hair to wipe them dry. You didnt give me a welcome kiss, but she keeps kissing my feet. There wasnt any oil for the head either, but she has put myrrh on my feet. So let me tell you, she did do many things she shouldnt have, but all are forgiven because she loved so much. Someone let off less wont have so much love. And Jesus told the woman Your sins are forgiven.

        bigger debtor, more obliged
        loved more, forgiven more   PVAJUY.XR

11. Gospel Comparisons – Luke

8.4 parables   Sower   K4, M13 : 90

This farmer was out sowing, and some seed fell on the path and got trodden in; along came the birds and ate it up. Other seed fell on a stony place and did show up but then dried off for lack of moisture. Some fell among thistles, which came up and throttled it. But some fell on good ground and grew up and swelled and gave a crop, yielding a hundredfold. And he said Anyone with ears had better listen.   (8.11 explains)

Some seed lost, but harvest great
same goes for preaching too   .   SOE.TC

8.16   lamp   K4, M5 : 94

No-one lights up a lamp to stick under a bucket or underneath the bed. It goes on the lampstand, so anyone coming in can see the light.

lights are to see by
so are parables   PAO.D/mB

10.2 preaching mission   send more men   M9 : 139

How great is the harvest, how few there are to gather it! Better ask the boss to send more men, for harvesting.

need more harvesters
only God supplies preachers   POEU.D

How Parables Work

10.29 lawyer's query   <u>Good Samaritan</u>   : 144

Keen to put himself in the right, the lawyer asked Jesus Who is my 'neighbour', then? Jesus took him up on that. This chap was going down from Jerusalem to Jericho, and got ambushed by robbers. They took his clothes, beat him up, and went off leaving him half dead. A priest happened to come down that way, took one look at the fellow and kept going. A Levite also came along, saw how things were, and carried on. Then a journeying Samaritan came there, saw the man and took pity on him; bandaged his wounds with oil and wine, set him on the donkey and took him to an inn and saw to him. Next morning he gave the innkeeper two pounds saying Please look after him. If you spend more I will repay you when I come this way again. So which of these three would you say was a neighbour to the one who got mugged? The one who took pity on him, said the lawyer. On your way, then, said Jesus, and mind you do the same.

> *the foreigner was neighbourly*
> you be like that foreigner   SVAJU.XR

11.5 Lords prayer   <u>Keep Knocking</u>   : 147

Suppose you go round to a friend's, late at night, to beg three loaves of bread, as a guest has turned up and you dont have anything to offer him. And your friend says Leave it off. The door is locked. My children are in bed with me. There's no way I can get up and give you bread.

11. Gospel Comparisons – Luke

Yes but - says Jesus – while friendship may not get him out of bed, shame will. It will get him up and make him give you all you ask.

 he'll have to get up in the end
 in the end, God *will* answer prayer   SWYO.D

11.10   <u>snake sandwich</u>   M7 : 148

Every asker gets, every seeker finds, the door always opens if you knock. If your son asks for fish will you give him a snake? Or a scorpion, when he asks for an egg? Rotters you may be, but you do know what is good for your kids; and wont your father in heaven give holy spirit to those who ask him for it?

 won't give your kid one
 God's an even better giver   PWJUE.D

11.14 devil's help <u>divide and ruin</u>   K3, M12 : 149

He cured a dumb man. Who actually spoke, when the devil came out. The crowd were stunned; but same said Beelzebub the chief devil must be helping him. Others tried to test him, asking for a sign from heaven. He could see their drift all right. He said, A kingdom torn by civil war cannot survive, nor can a family. Satan's rule would be finished, if he fought against himself. And by the way, if I had help from the devil, who is helping your people? Ask them! But if God is lending me a hand, then his kingdom has arrived, and you never realised.

 division weakens, fatally
 Satan divided is Satan finished   PWJ.XR/1ClmE

11.21   <u>first subdue</u>   K3, M12 :149

Property guarded by a tough guy keeping watch in armour should be safe. Unless a tougher guy beats him up, strips off his armour and gives his weapons away as spoil.

         first beat up householder
         Satan is beaten now   PWO.X

11.24   <u>Vacant Possession</u>   M12 : 150

When the foul spirit leaves a man he strays round waterless places, finding no place to stay. Back he goes to the house he was in before, and finds it all swept, clean and tidy. So he rounds up seven other spirits, even naughtier, and they all come there to squat. So that man is even worse off than he was before.

         tenants bad, squatters worse
         [not a comparison?]   SJY.N/1O

11.29 sign please   <u>men of nin</u> + <u>Q of south</u>   M12 : 152

What a rotten lot you are! Sign-grubbing? Here's Jonah's, it's all you'll get. He was a sign to the Ninevites, as the Son of man will be for you. The Queen of the South will give evidence against you, on Judgment Day; for she came from the ends of the earth to hear Solomon's wisdom; and someone greater than Solomon is here now. The men of Nineveh too will show you up, having repented at Jonah's message; and someone greater than Jonah is here now.

         repented at Jonah's call
         travelled far to hear Solomon
         you lot didn't   PJU,TZ/mXR

11. Gospel Comparisons – Luke

11.34   <u>eyelights</u>   M6 : 153

The eye lets light into the body; a clear eye lights up the whole body but a bad one leaves it in the dark. So dont let your light go out on you. Now if your body is all lit up, with no darkness anywhere, it'll all shine out, like a lightning-flash which shows you your way.

all you have to see with
<X is all you have to Z with, so ..>   PWAOU.D/lT

12.13 legacy   <u>Bigger Barns</u>   : 156

Someone called from the crowd, Teacher, ask my brother to share the inheritance with me. Jesus said Who made me a judge or arbitrator over you? And he told them all, Dont be grabbers. Life isn't just having lots of things. And he told them a parable. This rich man had a really bumper crop, one year, and nowhere to put it all. What to do, he wondered. I know, I'll dismantle my barns and put up bigger ones to store all my corn and stuff. Then I can have a proper holiday. With all that in store, it should last for years. Come on, you can eat, drink and enjoy yourself. But God thought different. You twerp, its tonight they're coming for your soul. And whose will all that stuff be then? Which goes for anyone saving up just for himself instead of being well off for God.

death upset his selfish plans
not a comparison?   SJF.XRC

How Parables Work

12.35 dont worry   <u>Night Out</u>   : 158

Keep your boots on and your lanterns lit, like chaps waiting up for their boss to come back from a wedding, so they can open up at once when he comes and knocks. Those servants who are up and awake will really find it made; he'll sit them down and come in an apron to wait on them – even if he comes home very late.

*   wait up for the boss*
*   you be all ready for him*   SYB.EU

12.39   <u>burglar</u>   M24 : 158

Had the owner known when the burglar would come, he could have stopped him breaking in. And you must be ready for the Son of Man's turning up, any time.

*   dont know when he'll come*
      YOU BE READY FOR THE SON OF MAN   PWAJUY.D/1C

12.42   <u>Two Stewards</u>   M24 : 158

Peter asked Was that aimed at us? Jesus answered This faithful and sensible servant was put in charge of the others, to give out their rations. Which will pay him, if its still true when the boss comes back. He'll put him in charge of everything! But suppose he thinks The boss is taking his time, and starts bullying the boys and girls, with feasting and drunken parties all day long! His boss is going to turn up unexpectedly, carve him up and chuck him out to join moaners and groaners outside.

*   boss will come and sort them out*
*   so will God*   SWYO.D

11. Gospel Comparisons – Luke

12.47   beaten less   : 159

Neither Bill nor George did what the boss wanted; Bill unintentionally, but George quite knowingly. Both got a walloping, of course, but George got a better one. People expect more from you, if you were given more.

    disobedience worse, if deliberate
    <some had Law, so less excuse>   POF.XR

12.54 peace?   signs of times   M16 : 160

When you see cloud building in the west you say a shower's coming, and so it does; and when a gale blows from the south you declare a heatwave is on its way. What clowns you are, so knowing about earth and sky, so ignorant of the way things are going herebelow.

    you forecast weather
    why not events?   PU.X/1

12.57   last farthing   M 5 : 161

Cant you decide what is right, on your own? Try to come to terms with your opponent while on your way to court. Otherwise he may carve you up before the judge; and the judge will pass you on to the jailer and the jailer will stick you in jail. Once there you wont get out, I promise you, till the very last penny has been paid.

    settle out of court
    no comparison?   PYO.TN/mD

How Parables Work

13.6 pilate's massacre   <u>Figs Last Chance</u>   : 162
This chap had a fig in his vineyard. He came for the fruit, but found none. So he said to the man Its three years now I've been coming for the fruit, but never got a single fig. Chop it down! It's taking up good ground. But the man said Sir, just let it go on one more year. I'll dig around and manure it, that may make it yield. If not, you can cut it down.

        give it one last chance
        <that's what you're getting>   SO.RC

13.18 sabbath heal?   <u>mustard</u>   K4, M13, : 164
A comparison for God's rule. Think of a mustard seed. This chap sowed it in his plot, and it grew up like a tree and the birds took shelter among its branches.

        tiny seed, big bush
        kingdom could grow like that   POH.D/kmC

13.20   <u>yeast</u>   M 13 : 164
God's kingdom? This woman took some yeast and mixed it with three measures of wheat flour, until all of it was leavened. There you have it.

        leavens the lot
        kingdom pervasive   PWOH.D/mC

11. Gospel Comparisons – Luke

13.25 few saved? <u>Locked Out</u> : 165

That door's narrow, a real struggle to get through. Which many try, but few succeed. Its like a feast, when the owner gets up and locks the door, and you're standing there outside, knocking and shouting Sir open up for us. No, he says, I dont know who you are. So you start to explain, You were there when we took our meals, you gave your message in our town square. But he will say I dont know where you're from. *Get away from me you criminals!* That's when the wailing and groaning will begin; for you'll see Abraham and Isaac and Jacob and all the prophets in God's kingdom, and you lot chucked out. Folk will come from east and west, from north and south and sit down to feast in the kingdom. Which shows how those at the back may end up at the front, and leaders land up in the tail.

cant talk your way in
now, or then   SJUF.QX

14.1 Sabbath healing? <u>your ox</u> M 12 : 168

A sabbath dinner, this man with the dropsy turns up, so Jesus asks the lawyers and Pharisees, Is it OK to make someone better, on Sabbath? No reply. So he took the sick man and healed him and sent him off. And to them he said If your son or your ox fell down the well, you'd pull him out straight away, wouldn't you, even on Sabbath? They were lost for words.

you 'd rescue on Sabbath
doing good on sabbath is OK   PWBUY.TR/lE

215

14.7   <u>Top Table</u>   : 169

Watching them bagging the best seats, he offered a parable. When called to a wedding dont take the top seat, in case someone grander comes, and you are asked to give up your place and move down to the bottom end. What an embarrassment! Its better to start down there, then your host will say My good friend, please take a higher place – improving your prestige with all the other guests. For any self-promoter is heading for demotion, and any self-humbler will get promoted after all.

    try slumming to get promoted
    not a comparison   SOFU.XCN

14.12   <u>cant repay</u>   :169

And he said to his host, When you are having a party dont invite your friends and your brothers, your relations or rich neighbours, for they may then invite you back, and that will square up your account upstairs. If you do have a feast, invite beggars and those who are disabled, lame or blind, then you'll earn a real blessing, for they can't invite you back. Which means you are guaranteed a refund, when the good people all come back to life.

    parties for the penniless
    not a comparison   POY.XRN

11. Gospel Comparisons – Luke

14.15   <u>Missing Guests</u>   M22 : 170

Another guest hearing this said What a blessing, to have a meal in God's kingdom! Jesus said This chap got up a big party, with a long list of guests. Then he sent his servant round to say Please come, it's all ready. But each and every one began offering apologies. One said I have bought a field and I simply must go and inspect it. Please excuse me. Another said I've bought five sets of cart-oxen and I'm just on my way to try them out. Please excuse me. Another said I've just got married, that's why I cannot come. The servant went back and repeated all this to his boss. He got mad. Go out quickly, he said, into the squares and alleyways of the city and bring back the poor, the disabled, the blind and the lame. Which he did, and reported Sir, I did what you said but still there is room. And the boss said Go out to the roads and hedgerows and make them come in, so my house may be full. Those first invited are not going to get even a taste of my dinner.

No-shows replaced by will-go's
Same goes for kingdom-feast   SO.X/lR

14.27 discipleship   <u>cost to build, of war</u>   : 171

Bring your gibbet along, if you want to follow me. Suppose you decided to build a tower, wouldnt you do your sums first, to make sure that you could finish it? Just imagine, if you laid the foundations and then ran out of cash, everyone would be ribbing you 'This chap began building but he couldnt finish'. Or suppose a king was marching out to battle with another one, won't he work out first whether his ten thousand men can take on twenty

217

thousand from the other side? And if not, he'll send word asking for terms, long before the armies meet? That goes for you too: you can kiss goodbye to all you have or hold dear, if you want to be my follower.

    do your reckoning first
      before joining me   PWJ.TZ

14.34   <u>salt</u>   K9, M5 : 171

Salt is a fine thing - while it keeps its taste. Once that goes, there's no remedy. Its no good for field or dungheap. People just chuck it out. Now, if you do have ears, you listen good.

    cant re-saltify stale salt
    <and not only salt>   POUY.D/kJ

15.3   dont despise   <u>Lost Sheep</u>   M 22 : 172

Complaint: he keeps company with sinners and even eats with them. Jesus' reply: Suppose you had a hundred sheep and lost one of them, wouldn't you leave the others in the wilderness and go off searching until you found it, and then carry it home in glee and call friends and neighbours in to celebrate, saying I've found that sheep which was lost! And up in heaven they'll be partying over for one sinner who found repentance, not over ninety-nine others, who had no need of it.

    big party ,when found
    God keen not to lose any   SWAJ.DZ/lXC

11. Gospel Comparisons – Luke

15.8   Lost Coin   :172

Think of a woman whose entire wealth is just ten pounds. She loses one. Wont she get a lamp and sweep the house and turn it upside down till she finds it? And then she'll call friends and neighbours in, to celebrate: I've found that pound I lost. Which is how God's angels rejoice over one sinner who repents, honest it is.

    big party ,when found
    God keen not to lose any   SWAX.ZC

15.11   Prodigal   : 173

This chap had two sons. The younger one asked for his share of the family property, so the father divided what he had between them. Soon after, he got everything together and went abroad, far away; and all he had soon went on loose living. Then a hard famine struck that country, and he was really hard up. He went to work for one of the people there, who sent him out to lead the pigs around to find their food. He would have been glad to get stuffed on the nuts the pigs were eating, but no-one gave him any. That really brought things home to him, for he thought My father's workmen all have bread in plenty, and here I am near dead with hunger. I shall go back and say to him, Father, I have sinned against God and against you as well. I dont deserve to be called your son. Please take me on as one of your hired men. So off he went, and made his way home. Now his father spotted him some way off, and feeling sorry ran to meet him with a hug and a kiss. So the son said his piece: Father, I have sinned against God and you and no longer deserve to be called your son. But the father called the servants, Bring a robe quickly and put it on him, and a ring for his finger and shoes for his feet. And bring the calf we were feeding up for a feast, and butcher it so we may eat and enjoy, for this son of mine, who was dead, has come back to life, he was lost but now he is found. So the party began.

Now the elder son was away on the farm. And when he got near he heard music and dancing, and asked a servant what was going on. He replied Your brother has come, and your father has butchered that calf which was being fattened up, because your brother came back in good health. That made the elder brother wild, and he wouldnt go in to the feast. So his father came out, to persuade him. But he said See how long I've been slaving for you, always doing what you said, and not given even a kid, to have a party with my friends. Now this son of yours comes back, having run through your money on prostitutes, all of it, and you butcher the fattened calf for him! The father replied My boy, you are here with me all the time, and all I have will come to you. We had to throw a party for your brother, who was dead but came back to life, lost then but now is found.

      join party for long-lost son's return
      <another party for sinners returned>   SO.X

11. Gospel Comparisons – Luke

16.1 <u>Smart Manager</u> : 174

This rich man's manager was accused of waste. He called him and said What's this I hear about you? Let me see your accounts, for you cant go on in that job. And the manager thought What on earth am I going to do? The boss is taking my job away. I dont fancy life as a beggar, and I cant work in the fields. I know what to do, so I have somewhere to go when I get turned out. And he called in those who owed money to his boss, and asked the first How much do you owe? A hundred measures of oil, he replied. Well, here's the receipt, sit down quick and make it Fifty. He put the same question to another, who replied A hundred measures of corn. Here, take the bill. Write Eighty. And that dishonest manager got top marks for quick thinking, from the boss; for worldly people are more on the ball than are sons of light. And you, by the way, had better pall up with Black Money, so that when things come unstuck they can welcome you to their permanent residence. One who deals honestly with small sums can be trusted with bigger ones; but one dishonest with Black Money can never be trusted with real gold. And if you cant to be trusted with Black money who will entrust the good stuff to your care?

quick thinking got him a place to stay
   you'll be needing one too   SAJEUF.D

16.13 two bosses M6 : 174

No servant can work for two bosses. He'll either hate A and take to B, or despise B and hold by A. You can serve God *or* Money, but not both.

> *cant serve both*
> not God *and* Money   PWAJU.D

16.19 law stands Tell my Folks : 177

This rich fellow had a fine old time: purple and linen clothing, parties every day. And beggar Lazarus lay at his gate, wishing the rich man's table-crumbs could fill his tum. And the dogs used to come and lick his sores. Now the beggar died and the angels took him to join Abraham. The rich man also died and was buried. While he was in torture downstairs he spotted Abraham far away, and Lazarus with him. So he shouted Father Abraham for pity's sake send Lazarus down to wet his finger and cool my tongue. I'm getting hell in this flame. Abraham replied My boy, just recall how you enjoyed the Good Life, and Lazarus the bad. Now he gets some relief, and you suffer pain. In any case there's a great big gap between us; we cant cross to you, and you cant join us over here. Then the man said Father, would you kindly send Lazarus to see my family, and explain things to my five brothers there, so they dont land up in this hell-hall. Well, they've got Moses and the Prophets, they could try obeying them. Maybe not, father Abraham, but they would repent if someone came back from the dead. I doubt that. If the

11. Gospel Comparisons – Luke

whole Bible cant get them to obey, then nothing will, not even a dead man coming back to life.

They ignore scripture
so do you   SO.T

17.7 faith, please   <u>Only Doing Job</u>   : 181
When your man comes in from ploughing or shepherding, do you say Here, take a seat and have dinner? No, you say Cook something for me, then put an apron on and serve my meal. You can have yours afterwards. No-one thanks a servant for doing what he's told. And what about you? Well, do what you've been told, and then say We're only servants, not very good ones, we just did our job.

obedient slaves expect no thanks
nor should you   SWAJU.D

17.26 Son of man's day
           <u>noah's day / sodom folk</u>   M24 : 184
It'll be like old Noah's time, people went on eating and drinking and getting married until the day Noah boarded the ark, and the flood came and killed them all. And in Lot's time too people were eating and drinking, buying and selling, planting crops and building houses, until the day Lot left Sodom, then fire and brimstone rained from the sky and killed them all. That's how it will be when the Son of man stands revealed. Anyone up on the terrace when that happens should not stop to collect his things, and

someone out in the field had better not come home. Dont forget what happened to Lot's wife.

> *never saw flood coming*
> */carried on as normal*
> caught out on big day   PBJU.DZ

18.2 keep praying   <u>Persistent Widow</u>   : 185
A parable to help us keep praying and not give up. This judge in Somewheretown had no fear of God and took no notice of what people said. But one widow kept coming back to court saying Give me justice against my opponent. And he was damned if he would. But later on he thought Though I dont fear God or bother with man, even so I'd better give her justice. She's such a bother, in the end she'll do me in. And the Lord said Listen to this wicked judge. And wont God, who has been patient so long, give his chosen ones justice at last, as they cry to him day and night? Yes he will. It wont be long. Though when the Son of man comes will he find faith on the earth?

> *bad judge grants petition*
> God will do better   SYJE.XC

18.9 self-righteous   <u>Two Men Pray</u>   : 186
A parable for those who think they are good and despise others. Two men went up to the temple to pray, a Pharisee and a taxman. The Pharisee stood there saying in silent prayer I thank you God that I'm not like other folk, thieves for example, wicked people, adulterers or, indeed, this taxman here. I fast two days in seven, and pay tithes on

11. Gospel Comparisons – Luke

everything I have. But the taxman stood far away, not raising his eyes to heaven but just thumping himself and saying Dear God do have mercy on this sinner. And that man's prayer was heard, I assure you, but not the Pharisee's. Go-getters are sure to take a tumble, and those who take a lower path will get moved up.

> *one asked forgiveness*
> *and got it*   SYOEF.XC

19.11 kingdom now?   <u>Your Money Back</u>   M25 : 195

He was getting near Jerusalem, and they thought God's kingdom was about to be revealed. Hence this parable. This well-to-do chap was offered the kingdom of a faraway country, and had to go there to accept it, then come home again. Calling ten of his servants he gave each one a pound saying You trade on this till I come back. Now his countrymen did not like him at all, and they sent a messenger after him to say We dont want him as our king. When the man had accepted the kingdom and got back home, he sent for the servants he had given money to, to see how they got on. The first one said Sir I have made ten pound's profit with that pound of yours. Good, he said, you're an excellent servant, trustworthy even in small matters, come, you can take charge of ten cities. The second one said Sir with your pound I earned five more; and he was asked to take charge of five cities. Then the other chap came and said Sir here is your pound. I had it wrapped in a cloth and put away, for I was afraid. I knew you were a tough one, taking what is not yours, reaping

How Parables Work

where you had not sown. The man replied You've said it, you wicked servant, you've condemned yourself. You knew I was a tough one, did you, one who takes other people's stuff, reaping where I had not sown? Then why didn't you give the money to bankers, and I could have had it back with interest? So he gave orders to take the pound off him and give it to the first man, who had ten. And the people said Sir, he has ten already. Yes indeed. You see its havers that get and have-nots who lose what little they had. But bring here those enemies who did not want me to be their king, and slaughter them right here in front of me.

loan is not for burying
<nor is Israel's Special Relationship>   SYOEF.T/lC

20.9 by what right?   <u>Tenants Kill</u>   K12, M21 : 204
This chap planted a vineyard, fenced it, dug a well and built a tower, then let it off to tenants. At harvest-time he sent a man to collect his share of the crop, but they gave him a good beating and sent him back empty-handed. He sent another man, who also got thumped disgracefully. Yet another, who was wounded, then thrown out. The owner had only one left, his favourite son, so he sent him last of all, thinking 'surely they will respect my son'. But those tenants thought otherwise: 'here is the heir' they said, 'come on, let's kill him and we can keep the land'. So they killed him and threw his body out of the vineyard, unburied.

11. Gospel Comparisons – Luke

What is the owner going to do? He will come and destroy those tenants, and re-let the vineyard to others. No, they said, please, not that.

> *Owner will punish them and re-let*
> this government is on the way out SVAO.TC

21.29 Son of man's day   <u>signs of end</u>   K13, M24 : 220
Learn this lesson from the fig. When its branches are supple and the leaves come out you know summer's just round the corner. And when these things start happening you will know God's kingdom is very near. All these things are going to happen in my lifetime or yours. And what I say will outlast heaven and earth.

> *fig shows summer coming*
> these events show End is near   PJU.CD

Table 9   Coding

Definable features found in the comparisons are here coded. For a comparison found more than once, the common features are shown first and those special to one gospel come after / (with k or l or m).

PICTURE-PART
S tory
P icture
W ho, If, etc
V erdict asked for
A nswered with Verdict
U, hearers called 'you'
Y ou I'm telling, emphasis

REALITY-PART
J udgment given
O mitted judgment
B egan with judgment
E xplained, introduced
H, offered as likeness
F inished, moral as cap

A dot separates these features from context etc (below)

CONTEXT in Gospel
D isciples taught
T eaching in public, 'crowd'
X, named persons, group
R eplying

GENERAL
C alled 'parable'
Q uashed up, compressed
Z, twinned, one of pair
N on-comparison ?

This coding may be copied or developed without special permission.

Lists

beaten less	POF.XR
Bigger barns	SJF.XRC
blind leader	PWAO.D/lC
burglar	PWAJUY.D/lC
cant repay	POY.XRN
cost to build /war	PWJ.TZ
divide & ruin	PWJ.TR /kClmE
dont need doctor	PAJ.TR.
doorman	PJU.D
eyelights	PWAOU.D/lT
fast later	PAO.TR
Figs last chance	SO.RC
first subdue	PWO.X
food and dirt	PWJE.QT.C
found treasure/pearl	POH.DZ
gods garden	PO.D
Good Samaritan	SVAJU.XR
Half-day work	SOHF.T
Keep knocking	SWYO.D
kids at play	PJHF.T
lamp	PAO.D/mB
last farthing	PYO.TN/mD
Locked out	SJUF.QX
log in eye	PWAOU.D
Lost coin	SWA X.ZC
Lost sheep	SWAJ.DZ/lXC
Mean debtor	SBH EUD
men of nin/Q of S	PJU.TZ/mXR
Missing guests	SO.X/lR
mustard	POH.D/kmC
new & old	POH.D
Night out	SYB.EU

229

How Parables Work

noahs day	PBJ.DZ
Only doing job	SWAJU.D
Persistent widow	SYJE.XC
pig food	POU.D
Prodigal	SO.X
salt	POUY.D/kJ
seed	POH.D
send more men	POEU.D
Sheep and goats	SOU.DN
signs of end	PJU.CD
signs of times	PU.X/lT
Smart manager	SAJEUF.D
snake sandwich	PWJUE.D
sodom folk	PBJU.DZ
sorting fish	PJH.D
Sower	SOE.TC
spoilt coat/bottle	PWO.XZ/lC
Tell my folks	SO.T
Ten girls	SOHF.D
Tenants kill	SVAO.TC
Top table	SOFU.XCN
trees & fruit	PWJU.D/lO
two bosses	PWAJU.D
two builders	PBH.D
two debtors	PVAJUY.XR.
Two men pray	SYOEF.XC
two shopmen	POE.D
Two sons	SVAJUY.XR.
Two stewards	SWYO.D
Vacant Possession	SJY.N/lO
Weeds	SOHE.DC
yeast	PWOH.D/mC
Your money back	SYOEF.T/lC
your ox	PWBUY.TR/lE

Lists

Table 10   Comment

A few comments have been offered, on particular parables. These are noted here by chapter and section. But reference is not made to the *surveys* in chs.1, 3+4, nor to a parable cited as *example* for some point of theory.
Further information and suggestions can be found in commentaries. Try Dodd, Jeremias, Westermann, Hunter, or (in German) Harnisch or Weder.

beaten less 6.2	Mean Debtor 10.7
Bigger barns 8.4	men of Nin + 2.6
blind leader 7.5	Missing Guests 1.10, 8.3
burglar 6.5, 10.3	Prodigal 8.3
cant repay 8.7	salt 8.7
divide & ruin 7.1	Sheep & Goats 8.7
eyelights 8.7	Smart manager 6.2
fast later 7.5	Sower 5.4
Figs last chance 8.7	Spoilt coat + bottle 8.7
first subdue 1.8	Tell my folks 8.7
food and dirt 2.7	Tenants kill 7.6
found pearl + 10.6	Top Table 8.7
gods garden 7.5	two builders 6.1
Good Samaritan 8.5	two debtors 4n
lamp 6.2	Two men pray 7.5
last farthing 2.8, 8.7	Vacant possession 8.7
Locked out 2.9	yeast 9.2
Lost Sheep 3.1	Yr Money Back 7.5, 8.7
	your ox 4n

Table 11   Books +

giving details of those mentioned (mainly in the Notes).

Book-titles are shown in italics. So are names of journals.

For a listed item from a book, that book also is listed, by editor

A place-name may suggest a University Press.

&   means another work by the same author.

The, of, for   get left out.

Some recurrent words may get initialized:-

        B   ible, B iblical
        G   ospel
        J   ournal
        N   ew
        P   arable
        S   tudy
        T   estament

Lists

Anderson JC & Moore SD *Mark and Method*
        175 Fortress 1992

Bailey KE *Poet and Peasant*
        238 Eerdmanns 1976

Bailey JL & Broek LDv *Literary Forms in New T,*
        219 SPCK 1992

Barton J *History and Rhetoric in the Prophets,*
        in Warner, 51

&   Reader-Response Criticism,
        Expository Times. 2002, 147

& *Cambridge Companion to B Interpretation*
        338 Cambridge 1998

Beardslee WA Uses of Proverb in Synoptic G,
        Interpretation 1970, 61

Beavis MA Power of Jesus' Parables
        JStNT 2001, 3

Blomberg CL *Interpreting Parables*
        334 Apollos 1990

Bowker J *Targums and Rabbinic Literature*
        380 Cambridge 1969

Brown RE, Parable and Allegory Re-Considered
        Num Tum 1962, 36

&   *Introduction to the New Testament*
        878 Doubleday 1997

Bultmann R *History of the Synoptic Tradition*
        456 Oxford 1963

Bultmann R *Jesus Christ and Mythology*
 95 SCM 1958
Cadoux AT *Parables of Jesus, their Art and Use*
 255 J Clarke c1930
Caird GB *Language and Imagery of the Bible*
 280 Duckworth 1980
Calvert DGA ...criteria for ..words of Jesus
 NTSt 1971-72, 209
Clines D Deconstructing ... Job
 in Warner *Bible as Rhetoric*, 65
Crossan JO *Four other gospels*
 208 Winston 1985
& Parables of Jesus
 Interpretation 2002, 246
Daube D, Nathan's Parable
 N T um 1982, 275f
& *The New Testament and Rabbinic Judaism*
 460 London 1956
Delamont S *Interaction in the Classroom*
 160 Methuen 1976
Derrett JDM *Jesus' Audience*
 240 DLT 1973
Derrett *Law in the New Testament*
 500 DLT 1970
Detweiler R & Robbins VK Cxx Hermeneutics,
 in Prickett, 225
Dibelius M *From Tradition to Gospel*
 311 James Clarke 1934

Dodd CH *Parables of the Kingdom*
                                    214 Nisbet 1935
&   *Interpretation of the Fourth Gospel*
                                    475 Cambridge 1958
Donahue JR *Gospel in Parable*
                                    254 Fortress 1988
Drury J *The parables in the gospels*
                                    180 SPCK 1985
Evans CF *Parable and Dogma*
                                    20 London 1967
Farmer WR *Synoptikon*
                                    229 Cambridge 1969
Farmer WR *The Synoptic Problem*
                                    308 Macmillan 1964
Feldman A *Parables & Similes of the Rabbis*
                                    275 Cambridge 1927
Fish S *Is there a text in this class?*
                                    394 Harvard 1980
Foster L *Four for the Gospel Makers*
                                    127 SCM 1986
Fuller RH   *Crit Intro to New T*
                                    226 Duckworth 1966
Gerhardssohn B *Memory and Manuscript*
                                    379 Uppsala 1961
&   *If we do not cut the P out of their frames*
                                    NTSt 1991, 321
&   *Narrative Meshalim in Synoptic G*
                                    NTSt 1988, 339

Gillingham MJ Parables as attitude change
Expository Times. 1998, 297

Gospel of Thomas see Guillaumont

Goulder M, Characteristics of p in several G
JThS 1968, 51

    &   *A Tale of two Missions*
196 SCM 1994

Grant RM *Historical Introduction to the NT*
447 Collins 1963

    &   *Jesus after the gospels*
134 SCM 1990

Guillaumont A and others, *Gospel a/c Thomas,*
62 Collins 1959

Hanson RPC *Allegory and Event*
400 SCM 1959

Harnisch W Language of the Possible...
Studia Theologica 1992, 41

Harrison B *Inconvenient Fictions*
290 Yale 1991

Hendrickx H *Parables of Jesus*
291 Cassell 1986

Hengel M *Studies in the Gospel of Mark*
206 SCM 1985

Huck A *Synopsis of the first three gospels (in Greek)*
(and see Throckmorton*)*
213 Blackwell 1954

Hunter AM *Interpreting the Parables*
        126 SCM 1960

Iser W *Act of Reading*
        239 Routledge 1978

Jeremias J *Rediscovering the Parables*
        191 SCM 1966

&   *Parables of Jesus*
        248 SCM 1963

Jones GV *Art and Truth of the Parables*
        250 SPCK 1964

Kessler E *Radical Jesus in parables*
        Urban Theol. Unit, Sheffield 1985

Linnemann E *Parables of Jesus*
        216 SPCK 1966

Linton O ...Sayings and P in S G
        New T Studies 1980, 139

Lofland J ed, *Interaction in everyday Life*
        156 Sage 1978

Lowe M .....from order to Markan priority,
        N T um 1982, 27

Macphail JR P *of Jesus King and Teacher*
        84 CLS Madras 1976

Martin H P *of the G & Meaning For Today*
        254 SCM 1937

Martin WBW *Negotiated Order of... School*
        191 Macmillan 1976

Matarasso P trs *Quest of the Holy Grail*
        304 Penguin 1969

Metzger BM *NT Background, Growth...*
　　　　　　　　　　　　288 Lutterworth 1969
Miell D & Dallos eds *Social Interaction*　381 Sage 1996

Neill S *Interpretation of the New T 1861-1961,*
　　　　　　　　　　　　360 Oxford 1964
Pagels E　*Gnostic Gospels*
　　　　　　　　　　182 Weidenfeld & N, 1979
Palmer H　*Logic of Gospel Criticism*
　　　　　　　　　　　270 Macmillan 1968
&　　*Analogy: qualification ...theology*
　　　　　　　　　　　183 Macmillan 1973
&　　Just Married, Cannot Come
　　　　　　　　　　　N T um 1977, 241
&　　Stories
　　　　　　　　　Modern Theology 1986, 107
&　　Seeking Verdicts for Parables
　　　　　　　　　Expository Times. 2000, 262

Parker A *Painfully Clear*
　　　　　　　　　166 Sheffield Academic 1996
Patte D ed. *Semiology and Parables*
　　　　　　　　　　　384 Pittsburgh 1976
&　　*What is structural exegesis?*
　　　　　　　　　　　90 Fortress 1976
Patten P, Form and Function of P in apocalyptic
　　　　　　　　　　　NTSt 1983, 246
Peck J & Cole M *Literary Terms and Criticism*
　　　　　　　　　　　222 Macmillan 1984

Lists

Perrin N *Kingdom of God in Teaching of Jesus*
216 SCM 1963

    &   *Jesus and the Language of the Kingdom,*
225 SCM 1976

Plato *Republic*, trs. Cornford
356 Oxford 1941

Prickett S ed   *Reading the Text*
354 Blackwell 1991

Riesenfeld H, *Gospel Tradition*
30 Mowbray 1957

    &   *Gospels Remembered*
Oxford 1960, 147f.

Sanders EP ..Order and Relationship M - L
NTSt 1968, 249

Schadewalt W   Reliability of Synoptic Tradition
in Hengel, 85

Schweitzer *Quest of the Historical Jesus* 410
A&C Black 1910

Scroggs R Sociological Interpretation of N T
NTSt 1980 ,164

Streeter BH *Four Goospels*
226 Macmillan 1924

Shillington VG ed *Jesus and his Parables*
199 T&T Clark 1997

Teselle S M *Speaking in parables*
1975 S C M 186

Throckmorton BH,ed. *Gospel Parallels*
(Huck *englished*)   191 Nelson 1947

Thurber J *The Thurber Carnival*
405 Penguin 1945

Trigg R. *Tales Artfully Spun*
in Warner 117.

Warner M ed *Bible as Rhetoric*
236 Routledge 1990

Wenham D *Parables of Jesus*
272 Hodder & S 1989

Westermann C *Parables of Jesus in light of OT*
211 TTClark 1990

Wilson RM *Gnosis and the New Testament*
148 Blackwell 1968

Winton AP *Proverbs of Jesus*
236 Sheffield Academic 1990

Young B *Jesus and His Jewish Parables*
365 Paulist 1989

in other languages

Aland K *Synopsis quattuor evangelium*
                             590 Stuttgart 1964

Aurelio P Tullo *Disclosures in Gleichnissen Jesu*
                             360 Lang 1977

Fiebig P *Altjudische Gleichnisse & G Jesu*
                             166 Tubingen 1904

Flusser D *Rabbinischen Gleichnisse & .. Jesus*
                             1981 Lang 336

Harnisch W *Die Gleichniserzaehlungen Jesus*
                             326 Vandenhoek & R, 198

Kahler C *Therapeutische Wahrheit*
         in Franke H + *Veritas Et Communicatio* ,
                             Vandenhoek & R, 1995 , 19-39

Marion D   Simples et Mysterieuses Paraboles
                             Esprit et Vie (Lang) 1996, 105

Weber H *Die Gleichnisse Jesu als Metaphern*
                             312, Vandenhoek + R, 1978

More articles on the parables come out each year;
see *New Testament Abstracts,*
     or ATLA database (online, titles only).

Table 12 Parable Finder

beaten less	L 12.47	Only Doing Job	L 17.7
Bigger Barns	L 12.13	Persistent Widow	L 18.2
blind leader	M 15.14, L 6.39	pig food	M 7.6
burglar	M 24.42, L 12.39	Prodigal	L 15.11
cant repay	L 14.12	queen of south	M12.42 L11.31
cost of war	L 14.31	salt	K9.49, M 5.13, L14.34
cost to build	L 14.28	seed	K 4.26
divide & ruin	K3.24, M12.25; L11.14	send more men	M 9.37, L 10.2
dont need doctor	K 2.17 M 9.13, L 5.32	Sheep and Goats	M 25.31
doorman	K 13.33	signs of end	K13.28, M 24.32, L 21.2
eyelights	M 6.22, L 11.34	signs of times	M 16.2, L 12.54
fast later	K 2.19, M 9.15, L 5.34	Smart Manager	L 16.1
Fig's Last Chance	L 13.6	snake sandwich	M 7.9, L 11.11
first subdue	K3.27, M 12.2; L11.21	sodom folk	L 17.29
food and dirt	K 7.15, M 15.11	sorting fish	M 13.47
found pearl	M 13.45	Sower	K 4.3, M 13.1, L 8.4
found treasure	M 13.44	spoilt bottles	K 2.22, M 9.16, L 5.37
god's garden	M 15.13	spoilt coat	K 2.22, M 9.16, L 5.37
Good Samaritan	L 10.29	Tell My Folks	L 16.19
Half-Day Work	M 20.1	Ten Girls	M 25.1
Keep Knocking	L 11.5	Tenants Kill	K 12.1, M 21.33, L 20.9
kids at play	M 11.16, L 7.31	Top Table	L 14.7
lamp	K 4.21, M5.15, L 8.16	trees and fruit	M 12.33, L 6.43
last farthing	M5.25, L 12.57	two bosses	M 6.24, L 16.13
Locked Out	L 13.25	two builders	M 7.24, L 6.47
log in eye	M 7.3, L 6.41	two debtors	L 7.40
lost coin	L 15.8	Two Men Pray	L 18.9
Lost Sheep	M 18.12, L 15.1	two shopmen	M12.35, L.6.45
Mean Debtor	M 18.21	Two Sons	M 21.28
men of nineveh	M12.41, L11.32	Two Stewards	M 24.45, L 12.42
Missing Guests	M 22.1, L 14.16	Vacant Possession	M 12.43, L 11.24
mustard	K 4.30, M 13.31; L 13.18	Weeds	M 13.24
new & old	M 13.52	yeast	M 13.33 L 13.20
Night Out	L 12.35	Your Money Back	M 25.14, L 19.12
noah's day	M 24.37, L 17.26	your ox	M 12.11, L 14.53

Spare copy of Table 12: can be cut out for bookmark

beaten less	L 12.47	Only Doing Job	L 17.7
Bigger Barns	L 12.13	Persistent Widow	L 18.2
blind leader	M 15.14 ,L 6.39	pig food	M 7.6
burglar	M 24.42 ,L 12.39	Prodigal	L 15.11
cant repay	L 14.12	queen of south	M12.42 L11.31
cost of war	L 14.31	salt	K9.49 , M 5.13,L14.34
cost to build	L 14.28	seed	K 4.26
divide & ruin	K3.24,M12.25; L11.14	send more men	M 9.37, L 10.2
dont need doctor	K 2.17 M 9.13,L 5.32	Sheep and Goats	M 25.31
doorman	K 13.33	signs of end	K13.28, M 24.32,L 21.2
eyelights	M 6.22, L 11.34	signs of times	M 16.2,L 12.54
fast later	K 2.19,M 9.15,L 5.34	Smart Manager	L 16.1
Fig's Last Chance	L 13.6	snake sandwich	M 7.9, L 11.11
first subdue	K3.27,M 12.2; L11.21	sodom folk	L 17.29
food and dirt	K 7.15, M 15.11	sorting fish	M 13.47
found pearl	M 13.45	Sower	K 4.3, M 13.1,L 8.4
found treasure	M 13.44	spoilt bottles	K 2.22,M 9.16,L 5.37
god's garden	M 15.13	spoilt coat	K 2.22,M 9.16,L 5.37
Good Samaritan	L 10.29	Tell My Folks	L 16.19
Half-Day Work	M 20.1	Ten Girls	M 25.1
Keep Knocking	L 11.5	Tenants Kill	K 12.1,M 21.33 ,L 20.9
kids at play	M 11.16, L 7.31	Top Table	L 14.7
lamp	K 4.21, M5.15, L 8.16	trees and fruit	M 12.33, L 6.43
last farthing	M5.25, L 12.57	two bosses	M 6.24, L 16.13
Locked Out	L 13.25	two builders	M 7.24, L 6.47
log in eye	M 7.3, L 6.41	two debtors	L 7.40
lost coin	L 15.8	Two Men Pray	L 18.9
Lost Sheep	M 18.12, L 15.1	two shopmen	M12.35,L.6.45
Mean Debtor	M 18.21	Two Sons	M 21.28
men of nineveh	M12.41, L11.32	Two Stewards	M 24.45,L 12.42
Missing Guests	M 22.1,L 14.16	Vacant Possession	M 12.43, L 11.24
mustard	K 4.30, M 13.31; L 13.18	Weeds	M 13.24
new & old	M 13.52	yeast	M 13.33 L 13.20
Night Out	L 12.35	Your Money Back	M 25.14,L 19.12
noah's day	M 24.37,L 17.26	your ox	M 12.11, L 14.53

How Parables Work

www.ingramcontent.com/pod-product-compliance
Lightning Source LLC
Chambersburg PA
CBHW022005160426
43197CB00007B/281